the
Pantyhose craft book

the Pantyhose craft book

JEAN RAY LAURY and JOYCE AIKEN

Taplinger Publishing Company | New York

First Edition

Published in the United States in 1978 by
TAPLINGER PUBLISHING CO., INC., New York, New York

Published simultaneously in Canada by Burns & MacEachern, Limited

Library of Congress Cataloging in Publication Data

Laury, Jean Ray.
    The pantyhose craft book.

    1. Textile crafts. I. Aiken, Joyce, joint author.
II. Title
TT699.L38 1978   746   78-5001

ISBN 0-8008-6235-X (CLOTH)   ISBN 0-8008-6234-1 (PAPER)

All work in this book is by the authors, except
where other designers are credited. All black and white
photographs are by Joyce Aiken and color photographs
by Jean Ray Laury, unless otherwise noted.

Special thanks to our marvelous (and patient) models:
Joel Aiken, Kirsten Betak, Ritva Laury, Phyllis Neufeld,
Jill Rosenberg, Roger Toy, and Margaret Trembley

Designed by Mollie M. Torras

Contents

Illustrations in Color

Foreword

If Mount Everest is climbed "because it is there," then leftover nylon stockings have something in common with Everest. They're put to use "because they are there." They accumulate in plastic bags, drawers, and closets—not quite so devastated that they must be discarded, but not actually wearable, either.

Our thrifty ancestors made use of every scrap and tatter of material in a variety of ingenious ways, out of a necessarily frugal use of fabric developing patchwork and pieced quilts. The satisfaction of making something useful from cast-off material is still with us. We all experience a special pride in having created "something out of nothing."

Also with us today is our increasing awareness of the necessity to recycle. It makes sense. Recycling is becoming a way of life, permeating every aspect of daily living. Finally, creating from old material invites a playful approach and allows for humorous and experimental work, since the investment in materials is minimal.

Here (at last!) is the definitive word on how to recycle your pantyhose, how to give new life to the nylon stockings which have already served you for one round. Today's rug may simply be the reincarnation of yesterday's violet mesh hose. Tomorrow's stuffed toys may regenerate from today's office-beige stockings.

Some of the projects in this book are functional, some pure fan-

Margaret Trembley with her nylon soft-sculpture companion, Sister.
(Photo by Jim Walsh)

tasy. Whether funny, funky, or useful, they will help you get started. May you find as much satisfaction, laughter, and sense of accomplishment in recycling pantyhose as we did!

1.
Preparation

Cleaning and preparing pantyhose is a simple process, but an important one. Let stockings accumulate in paper bags, boxes, or plastic sacks until you have enough to make the sorting, washing, and bleaching worthwhile.

A small batch of nylon stockings can easily be washed by hand and hung up to air dry. But if you've accumulated enough stockings and pantyhose to make a full washload, by all means, do them in the washer. Set the machine for a regular wash cycle and use detergent. The stockings may tangle a bit in the machine but are easily separated later. From the washing machine the stockings can go directly into the drier for a ten-minute cycle—longer for pantyhose with heavy-weave tops. If you find your drier tangles the stockings too much, air them dry. It doesn't take much longer. To sanitize the stockings, when you do not wish to bleach them, add ½ of a cup of ammonia to the washing-machine water. Use less for hand washing. If you are bleaching the hose for dyeing, that will serve to cleanse them. Do not combine household bleach with the ammonia as it creates a dangerous gas.

SORTING

Sort through the different types of stockings you have. Some will be sheer, leg-length, and shaped to the foot, ankle, and leg. Separate those from pantyhose of sheer mesh that goes from toe to waist with unshaped leg sections. Other pantyhose may have a mesh leg with a heavy knit top. Put those all together. Each type can be used to special advantage in particular projects. If you cut the legs from the heavy knit tops of pantyhose, be sure to save the tops as they come in handy for some projects. Whenever you start on something new, check to see if you have enough of the right kind of hose.

DYEING

To get brilliant dyed colors it is essential that the stockings be bleached before they are dyed. Color remover (available where hot-water household dyes are sold) will take the color out of most stockings. Follow the directions on the package. Household bleach also works well and, though its odor isn't very pleasant, it is less offensive than color remover. A mixture of one gallon of water and ¾ of a cup of bleach will readily remove the color from stockings.

Put the stockings and the bleach mixture into a large pan and bring to a simmer on the stove. Do not crowd the stockings or they will not bleach evenly. In ten to fifteen minutes the stockings will turn a light yellow but will not become white. Because of variations in the original dye lots, the degree of bleaching is rarely identical from one pair of hose to the next. A few colors simply cannot be removed by bleaching. But this is no cause for concern. The slight variations in color of lightened stockings actually enhance the final color range.

Remove the stockings from the bleach and place in cool water with a small amount of detergent added to help remove the smell of bleach. Rinse thoroughly and air dry.

Regular household dyes will color nylon stockings very well. All the colored stockings used for projects in this book were dyed with household, hot-water dyes, such as Rit or Putnam, available in grocery and department stores. A concentrated amount of dye in a small amount of water yields the most intense color. Since dyes are transparent, you can dye one color over another for a new color, but only

A basketful of dyed nylons and pantyhose ready for use. (Photo by Jean Ray Laury)

going from lighter to darker colors. Yellow stockings dyed in a thin red dye solution will turn orange. The color of the stockings will always show through or somehow affect the dye color. A very intense, concentrated dye bath is required to cover an already-colored stocking. For varying shades of one color, dye a few stockings in the dye bath. Then remove them and add a few more. As the dye concentration is depleted, each new batch of stockings will come out lighter than the previous batch. You will produce a nice range of colors to choose from.

After completing the dyeing, rinse all dye from the stockings in cold water or put through a cold-water cycle in the washing machine. Dry by machine or hang to air dry. If it is necessary to wash a dyed project later, use a mild soap in cool water and wash separately.

CUTTING

Choose the appropriate type of stocking and cut it into strips or shapes as instructed for each project. The different weaves of each

Detail of crocheted shower rug of white cotton strips and beige and brown pantyhose strips, by Pauline Schwartz.

type of stocking react differently when cut. Some roll up into round strings, others stay flat and straight. Experiment with cutting before plunging into projects requiring a big pile of hose.

While you are washing, sorting, dyeing, and cutting, you will become familiar with the characteristics of the material. The nature of mesh as contrasted to the smooth hose will make certain uses obvious. While we were working on the projects for this book, we discovered what could and could not be done with pantyhose, and we developed various techniques for stuffing, padding, weaving, and quilting. These are described in detail in Chapters 6 through 9.

2.
Clothes and Accessories

The use of nylon hose in clothing ranges from the sublime to the ridiculous. While many practical uses of nylons are readily apparent, other, less functional, creations serve as humorous embellishments and fantasy pieces. Accessories may be as usable as totes, as nostalgic as garden-party hats, or as delightfully imaginative or absurd as novelty jewelry.

Coiled-Top Tote

The hopsacking shoulder tote has a colorful coiled pattern which creeps over the top of the bag and curls down the reverse side. Upholstery cording, 1/2 of an inch thick, was wrapped with strips of varying lengths of the heavily woven top portion of pantyhose. Each wrapped section was overcast-stitched on the back so that the wrapped nylons were firm and secure. After the cording was covered, it was whip-stitched to the purse flap. The cording gives a nice stiffness to the flap and makes it easy to lift when you want to rummage about inside.

Wrapped Scuffs

Luxuriously soft and comfortable, these scuffs are easy to make. First, trace around your foot to make a pattern. Cut the sole shape

Coils of dyed hose tops
of blues, yellows, reds, and
turquoises add a rainbow effect to
the off-white tote made
by Patt Rank.

These vivid red scuffs are soft and washable.

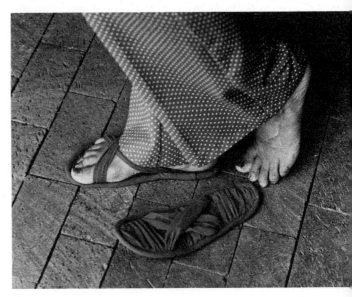

from a scrap of quilted fabric or any similar padded material. Then lay strips of dyed nylon stocking crosswise on the sole until it is entirely covered. Pin in place. Machine-stitch with a straight stitch at the outside edge of the sole. Trim next to the sole.

To make the straps, use the full width of the leg of a stocking and place it crisscross fashion over the top of your foot. Determine the proper length and the most comfortable positions for the two straps. Gather the ends of each length and pin them to the outside edge of the sole, raw ends meeting raw edges of the sole. Topstitch as in the drawing.

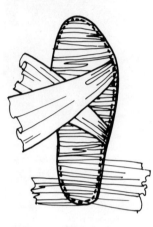

Topstitching the scuff

Next, cut a length of stocking about 2½ inches wide and long enough to go around the sole at the outside edge. Fold this strip lengthwise, and sew it to the top of the sole with the cut edges of the strip facing out and lined up evenly with the cut edge of the sole. Machine-stitch, covering the first line of machine stitching with this line. Then draw the folded edge over the raw outside edge of the sole. Whipstitch it to the bottom of the sole, trimming and tucking the ends in to make a smooth line.

Repeat these steps for the second scuff, being sure that you flip the pattern to make one right and one left foot.

Straw Hat with Roses

This hat has an air of luxuriant femininity with its soft roses and translucent band. Nylons dyed in reds and oranges are combined on the creamy-white hat. For the band, a sheer stocking is used—the kind that is shaped to fit the foot. It provides a band of color to which roses, made from a stretch-knit, sheer-mesh stocking, are attached. For directions for making the roses see Chapter 7.

Straw hat cradles
nylon-stocking roses
in its brim.

The band is drawn around the hat and the ends of the band are stitched together to secure them. Make the ends join where you are going to put the roses. On some hats it may be necessary to take a few catch stitches to secure the band to the hat. Then add the roses, using two or three tiny catch stitches to hold them next to the band, over the joined end.

Face Jewelry

Whole big bags of old nylons will never be consumed in jewelry making, but the stockings are an inexpensive material with which you can make some unusual rings and bracelets. While nearly all children delight in wearing this jewelry, some adults have also been known to have fun sporting these portable conversation pieces.

Using the directions in Chapter 6, make small stuffed-nylon-

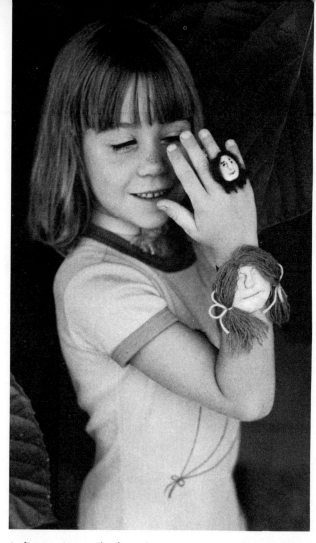

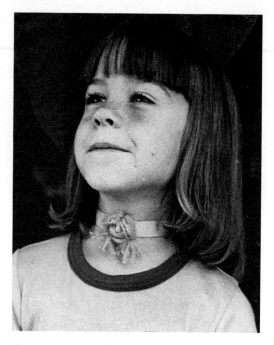

The face on this choker displays
an absurdly inviting smile.

A dinner ring and a bracelet more suitable for pot-luck
get-togethers than dinner at Maxim's.

stocking heads. They can be fully sculptured or bas relief on cardboard
forms.

Shops that supply jewelry findings usually have ring bases. Choose
one with a platform on which a stuffed head can easily be glued. The
bracelet here is a wristband of grosgrain ribbon with the stuffed face
sewn to it. Why not wear an entire family album, letting your hand
provide the gallery to exhibit your creations?

The choker is made in the same way as the bracelet, except on a longer ribbon.

Ponytail Posies

A small bouquet of roses adds delicate color and elegance to a simple hair style. These roses have centers of one color, with surrounding petals of a contrasting color. Each is made according to the instructions for the rosettes in Chapter 7. The three flowers are then stitched to a band of bright green nylon mesh which is tied to the hair.

Pale rosettes with multicolored centers are a piquant tie for a ponytail.

Denim puff tote does double duty in recycling jeans as well as nylons. 18 inches by 12 inches. By Bea Slater.

Denim Puff Tote

The soft faded tones of used denim offer a full range of blues in this sturdy, handsome bag. The individual puffs of this tote were made

On the reverse side, designer Bea Slater omitted the center panel and substituted the pocket section from blue jeans, making the tote easier to carry next to the body.

from muslin cut into 4-inch squares and denim cut into 6-inch squares.
This gives a finished 3-inch puff. To make puffs see Chapter 9. The puffs are joined to make rows of 3 puffs each and a total of 10 rows are used. Two rows are joined to make the center panel. Four rows are set in at each side, and they wrap around the ends. Puffs can be used in almost any tote pattern by simply substituting a section of joined puffs for a piece of fabric of equal size.

Grape-Cluster Comb

Puffs of Dacron batting are covered with purple mesh hose and clustered together to form a bunch of grapes over a comb. The individual grapes are sewn together and then attached to the comb with sewing thread. The leaves are made by forming florist's wire into the desired shape and then gluing a flat piece of green stocking over each. When the glue is dry, cut the excess nylon away from the edge and attach each leaf to the comb, tucked in with the grapes, with whipstitching. Tendrils are made from very pale green florist's wire and wrapped around one end of the comb.

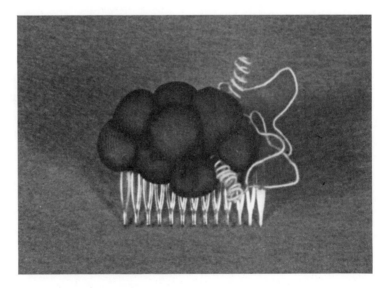

Grapes, complete with leaves and tendrils, are clustered on a small hair comb. By Patt Rank.

A bee and a snail emerge from wrapped cord and stretched nylon. By Patt Rank.

Bee and Snail Pins

Nylon-covered cording forms the bodies of the snail and the bee pins. Half-inch-wide strips of dyed nylon are wrapped over jute cord and lightly glued at each end to secure them. The cording is coiled in the desired shape and whipstitched together. Embroidery stitches form the mouth and eye on the snail and the eyes on the bee. The wings and antennae on the bee are made by the same method as the one used to make the leaves and tendrils on the grape-cluster comb. They are attached to the bee body by inserting the wire ends into the coils and fastening them with glue. Pin backings, available at hobby shops, are attached to the undersides of the creatures with sewing thread.

Flower Choker

The choker is a length of grosgrain ribbon to which a single elegant flower has been attached. The flower, in three colors, is an en-

Three shades of pink in a soft rosette on ribbon form a delicate choker.

larged version of the rosette. For making rosettes see Chapter 7. Mesh nylon was used in this example; the silky-textured hose will produce a softer, lighter, and floppier flower.

Braided Scuffs

The scuffs are made of braided nylons which are whipstitched together in precisely the method used in joining braided rugs. To make one, follow directions given in Chapter 8. The sole is made from 3-strand braids and the straps use 6-strand braids. When the braiding is wrapped so the sole is within one row of completion, stitch straps firmly to the outer edge of the sole. Then add the last row of braiding to the sole, covering the strap at each side.

Braiding makes a trim scuff.

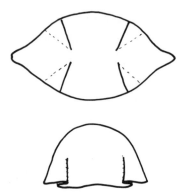

This Juliet cap recycles thread and yarn as well as the nylon hose that covers them.

Shape for the Juliet cap showing positions of the tucks

Stitched Cap

Peggy Moulton's creation is a soft Juliet cap. She used a fabric shape, cut as in the drawing, over which she spread a collection of colored threads, yarns, sewing table "sweepings," and soft pads of lint from the drier. Pantyhose nylon was spread out over this mass of threads and yarns and then heavily machine-stitched, forming a raised, quilted pattern over the entire surface. Tucks, taken at the sides, gave the hat its final shape. More machine stitching was added over the tucks.

Corded Necklace and Bracelet

Wrapped cording forms the basis of the necklace and bracelet. The necklace is made in two parts, with the circular neckband made of heavy wire that has been wrapped with nylon strips. The pendant portion of the necklace is made from wrapped jute, which makes a flexible coil which can be shaped as desired. Half-inch strips of dyed nylon are wrapped around the jute and lightly glued at each end to secure them. A little glue and an extra strip of nylon holds the pendant to the neckband.

The coil bracelet is made from one continuous length of nylon-covered cording stitched to a fabric bracelet form. The change in colors occurs with the change in the nylon wrapping. Since colors and coil sizes are identical, the bracelet and necklace, made by Patt Rank, are a matched pair.

Wrist Pincushion

The pincushion resembles a piece of jewelry but functions well as a holder of pins and needles. Penneye Kurtella used balls of cot-

Wrapped jute can be twisted into unusual shapes for a necklace, or whipstitched on straight as in the bracelet.

Cotton-stuffed nylon balls with imitation pearls form a modern version of the old-fashioned wrist pincushion.

ton batting covered with dyed stocking to form puffs that were incorporated into the pincushion. The puffs are sewn one by one to a padded backing which is attached to a wristband. Costume-jewelry pearls are stitched in between the puffs to finish off the decoration.

Textured Tote

Variously dyed nylon makes a shaggy, textured surface on this tote. A heavy fabric base is first cut in the shape of a large rectangle. It will later be folded in half to complete the tote. The rectangle is layed out flat and the hose strips are placed lengthwise on top. Single rows of machine stitching secure them to the tote material in lines sewn at intervals all across the surface as in the drawing. Hose can be cut off at any point and replaced with others of different colors to achieve a variegated effect. Clip some of the nylon when all the stitching is finished. The clipping forms a fringe. Some of the areas, left unclipped, will have a smooth, linear pattern. Then join the side seams with right sides together, and turn. Add handles and lining.

Machine-stitching the textured tote

Corded Serpentine Belt

The belt is made of wrapped cording. Patt Rank covered a length of cording with narrow strips of nylon stockings, using a carefully limited range of colors. The strips were wrapped on the cording and

Yellows, muted reds, lavenders, and taupes intermingle in this textured tote.

Strips of gold, orange, purple, mauve, and bronze tones were wrapped over cording which was then whipstitched to a felt background.

lightly glued at each end to secure them. She then whipstitched the cording, in a serpentine design, to a felt belting. One end of the cording on the belt forms a large loop that slips over a coiled button on the other end. The loop and button close the belt.

Garden Hat

This hat has a soft flower made in an unusual way. Cut a 5-inch-wide strip of nylon-stocking material of a summery pastel color. Fold it in half lengthwise. Sew along the cut edge and gather it as shown in the drawing. This will make a posy shape. Overlap the ends and cover the center with a large button, also covered in pantyhose nylon. A matching band of hose is wrapped around the crown of the hat.

A single nylon flower adds summer softness to a garden hat. By Patt Rank.

Making the flower for the garden hat

Stitching the halter top

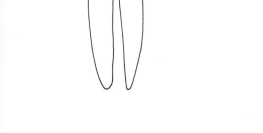

Colorful halter made from the legs of
stretch-knit pantyhose.

Midriff Halter

The halter is made from the legs which are cut off from two pairs of stretch-knit pantyhose. One leg is used to make the band which ties around the rib cage. Take two other legs and, measuring from the toe end, determine how long a strip is needed to tie them behind the neck. Join them to the midriff band in front, as shown in the drawing. Cut away any excess. The finished toe ends make a tie for the halter. For a larger bra top, use the upper portion of the hose, cutting off the foot section and knotting the cut end. Both ends of the hose are cut off for the section going around the ribs.

Swimsuit and Sunsuit

The sunsuit shorts are made by using two pairs of pantyhose, one over another, cut off about two-thirds of the way up the thigh. The

Sunsuit combines
hose of contrasting
colors into cuffed pants
and tied bra top.

raw ends are then rolled together to cover the raw edges. Cuffs are formed by folding the bottom color up over the top one.

The top is made from two legs. Determine the length needed to go around the body and tie in the back. Be sure to allow for some stretch. Then divide that length between two legs and cut any excess off the top end of each leg. Sew the open, raw ends of the hose together with a machine stitch, sewing back and forth several times to make the seam secure. Turn so that the seam is to the inside, then tie a short strip of hose of a contrasting color over this seam. That forms the deco-

strip of hose of a contrasting color over this seam. That forms the deco- rative line on the front of the sunsuit top. Toe ends of the stocking make the ties behind the back.

Blue Evening

Armed with scissors and a bag full of pantyhose, Phyllis Neufeld created a collection of instant clothing.

In the Blue Evening swimsuit, the top is made from the panty part of pantyhose. It is important that the pantyhose have a front and back center seam with an inset gusset section. To make the top, cut

Blue Evening swimsuit.

Orange Sherbet
trimmed with roses has
a matching turban.

the legs off about one inch below the heavy-weave part. Then remove the gusset inset by cutting just outside the stitch line. Pull the top on with the arms going through the leg openings. Stretch lace can be sewn in place around the neck opening.

The suit bottom is made using two pairs of pantyhose with the legs cut off, the legs of the darker, under pair 2 inches longer than the outer pair. It is this darker leg length that turns up over the outer panty leg to create a cuff of contrasting color. Another leg was used as a belt.

Orange Sherbet

In Orange Sherbet, Phyllis Neufeld made the suit bottom in olive green and orange in the same way she made Blue Evening. The top is a single orange stocking with the foot removed and the leg cut open to make a flat length. It is wrapped around the body and tied in back. The two legs, cut off the olive green pantyhose, have the feet removed and become the shoulder straps for the top. Roses made according to directions in Chapter 7 add a decorative flourish.

The head wrap is made from a regular leg-length stocking with the heavy-weave top. Phyllis pulled the heavy-weave section over her head with the leg section falling to the front. A second stocking in green was tack-stitched to the top of the cap with the leg section following the first one. The two are wrapped over one ear and tucked in at the back.

Puff Tote

The capacious hopsacking tote has a front panel of brightly patterned puffs. Lynda Fletcher made each puff finish at 2½ inches square. Muslin pieces were cut 3½ inches square and the print fabrics of con-

The puff tote is navy blue with brilliant cotton prints for puffs and lining.

trasting colors were cut into 5-inch squares. A single nylon stocking fills each. For directions on puff quilting see Chapter 9.

The finished puff panel is 15 inches across and 12½ inches high set into a navy blue tote. One of the printed fabrics is also used as a bright lining. This tote uses not only an entire drawer full of nylons, but scraps and remnants of fabric as well.

Rose Corsage

A single rose made in the same way as the rosettes in Chapter 7 is used to make a corsage. It is combined with leaves formed over thin cardboard. Follow directions for working on cardboard given in Chapter 6.

A large rose with leaves makes a corsage so lightweight it can be worn on any fabric. 6 inches long.

Flower Comb

Some shimmering, translucent flowers in gossamer oranges and yellows are attached to a comb as a hair ornament. These are double

Double flower comb by Patt Rank.

flowers made of nylon and florist's wire. Directions for making them are in Chapter 7.

It seems too obvious to mention, but nylon pantyhose with runs can be recycled as nylon pantyhose, too. Anyone who puts on a new pair of stockings at 7:00, only to snag them on a chair rung at 8:30, is eager to find a way to recoup her loss. There *are* ways of giving pantyhose new life . . . and of wearing them.

One can, first of all, mend a run with embroidery. It helps to slip a bottle or glass inside the stocking to make it easier to sew through just one layer of the nylon. First mend the hole or run with a single strand of matching thread. Use a whipstitch and catch each end of the run securely. Then get creative.

Two strands of embroidery floss give a strong color line. Ball-point needles will make the mending easier. An outline stitch works well for the embroidery, as does backstitch or featherstitch. Since nylons are semitransparent, all stitches used to embellish or repair them will show through the mesh. Therefore, in using something like French knots, remember that the lines connecting the knots will also show. Continuous-line stitches, such as outline and satin stitches, will avoid this problem.

Sometimes runs can be used in the design. A run that comes from the top could terminate in a tiny spider, painted or embroidered at the end of the run to prevent its traveling any farther. A run from the bottom can become the stem of a tiny decorative flower.

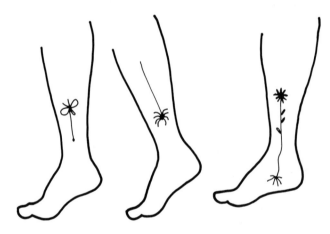

Suggested designs for embroidering runs

Acrylic paints can be used to add an embroiderylike decorative detail to hose. Again, it is important to have a glassy surface inside the stocking on which to paint. Any smooth-surfaced bottle or plastic container will do. The acrylic should be used straight from the jar or thinned only slightly. Opaque dots of the paint should sit on the surface of the nylon.

Hose can be successfully tie-dyed in brilliant colors. Small mends disappear completely in the face of such bright patterns.

Designs for painting or
embroidering runs

A final means of revitalizing pantyhose with just one little run is one used by many women. They select two pairs of pantyhose, one with a run in the right leg, the other with a run in the left, and cut the ruined leg off each. Then they recombine them. If beiges match, the hose appear as though they were meant for each other. If you use bright-colored tights, you can wear stockings of different colors (like a green and a blue, or a pink and an orange). This works well with solid-colored leotards.

3.

For the Home

Pantyhose can be used for a remarkable range of household accessories, from useful though decorative rugs, room dividers, window coverings, and place mats, to fantastic flowers and bouquets. Even three-dimensional forms of containers, sachets, and pincushions can be fashioned from hose. This chapter includes a variety of projects, many of which are surprisingly uncomplicated.

Room Divider

A large but easy-to-make project for the home is a room-divider curtain. Use the sheer, leg-length hose, and bleach and dye if desired. Choose one or more colors of yarn for wrapping the stockings. Drop a small Styrofoam ball into the toe end of the stocking. Wrap yarn over the heel shape by making a loop of yarn with end A of the yarn at the top of the wrap as shown in the drawing. Coil the yarn over the loop with each wrap of yarn right next to the last. Continue coiling to make a long smooth band of color, but do not cover the end of the loop. Put yarn end B through end of loop and pull end A up tight so end B is tucked inside coil. Clip off excess yarn on both ends. Continue wrapping at intervals of 5 or 6 inches, sometimes with beads, sometimes without. The lightness of the stocking puffs out between

Room divider of
coral-dyed nylon is
wrapped with brightly
colored yarn for
color accents.

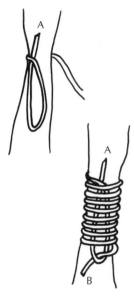

Wrapping the yarn for
the room divider

Detail of the room divider showing the wrapping of yarn.

wrappings and gives form to the stocking length. The wraps can be from 1 inch to 3 inches long. Complete the last wrap just before the heavy weave at the top of the leg.

If the opening to be covered by the curtain is longer than the length of one leg, it will be necessary to join one or more legs to the first. Take the toe ends of two wrapped legs and overlap the toes about 1 inch to ½ inch, and baste together. Now wrap yarn around the overlap being careful to cover all the heavy weave of the toes. Two legs will provide a length of approximately 6 feet. To join another leg to these, cut the heavy weave off the top of one of the joined stockings and overlap the toe of a new one to it in a manner similar to the joining described above.

When the correct length of wrapped stockings is achieved, flatten the stocking top and fold the double layer to the back, turning it down 1½ inches. Topstitch by hand or machine to make a channeling. Slip a metal or wooden rod into the stocking channels and install at the top of the opening you are going to cover. This allows the divider to move freely in a doorway or window. To weight the bottom edge, another rod can be slipped into a channel at the bottom of the wrapped lengths.

Fantasy Fern

The potted fern, in which fronds fall softly over a clay-pot base, is simple to make. A wire, cut about 12 inches long, makes the stem. A

The fronds of this fantasy fern are about 12 to 14 inches. By Patt Rank.

single layer of dyed mesh nylon is placed over the wire and glued on the wire. It is cut at the edges in a zigzag pattern suggesting the complex shape of a fern. All the stems are held together at the base and tied. Then the individual ferns are bent outward into a graceful arrangement. A gravel-filled clay flowerpot holds the tied stems upright.

Round Latched Rug

Sue Mathys, whose energy is equaled only by her supply of nylon hose, handcrafted this latched rug. The project was completed ten years ago and has been in constant use ever since. She bleached, then dyed the hose with regular household dyes. The rug has shown no signs of fading during these years. It is 9 feet in diameter and required 27 feet

Luxurious latch rug is 9 feet in diameter. (Photo by Sara Tanner)

of 40-inch-wide latch canvas cut into three equal lengths. The canvas pieces were overlapped 2 inches at the selvages and held together with 10-penny nails acting as straight pins while the design was drawn.

Sue then took the sections apart and worked on them individually, leaving the 2-inch margins to be worked later. She carefully set aside enough pieces of dyed stockings to match the design along the overlaps. One stocking covered about 4 square inches; one pair of pantyhose, 8 to 10 square inches.

After all three sections of the rug were latched (following the directions in Chapter 8), the 2-inch margins were overlapped and stocking pieces were latched through both thicknesses of canvas to complete and finish the rug. She recycled more than 3,000 stockings for this beautifully colorful and serviceable rug.

A rug like this makes a great family project and a walk-on heirloom.

Back of the rug shows the three sections of canvas joined at the selvages. A bias rug tape covers the hemline at the outside edges. (Photo by Sara Tanner)

Shaped Room Divider

Another room divider offers a dramatic pattern of circular forms. In this case it was used in a double glass doorway. Lengths of stretch-knit nylon are joined as described in the room divider at the beginning of this chapter. Then separate the parts of embroidery hoops to make two rings. You can use either plastic or wood hoops unless they have the metal clamps for tightening.

Insert hoops into the stockings. The nylon will draw tight between the hoops to create a variety of patterns. Be sure to stretch the nylons as they are being wrapped. The photograph shows the screen with the light coming from the outside so the transparent areas are soft in contrast to the linear patterns of the circles. When the light comes from the inside the nylon appears as opaque shapes. The lengths of stocking are stapled or tacked to the wood frame at top and bottom. The excess stocking is cut away so that the staples or tacks can be covered with a grosgrain ribbon, fabric braid, or a wood strip.

While embroidery hoops make excellent rings, a variety of other rings and discs can be substituted. The plastic lids of coffee cans make excellent discs. The larger sized ones may buckle if there is too much pull from a tightly woven stocking. You have to experiment to find the correct balance between the size of the disc and the hose density. Since some of these are colored it is possible to vary the color range by adding colored discs.

If you want to retain a transparent look, cut the centers out of the lids (using scissors) so that only the outer ring remains. The ring is not as rigid as the entire disc and some will be pulled into oval shapes which combine nicely with circles.

Many other kitchen items provide further rings and discs. Some take-out food containers have reinforced rims and will work well. Use a single edge razor blade or an X-acto knife to slice the rim off.

A dramatic translucent room divider
will also cover a glass door.

This pad of square knots makes a comfortable occasional pillow.

Many prepacked foods have round plastic lids which can be inserted in the stocking as they are.

Square-Knotted Pad

Here is a rug- and pad-making method devised especially for this book. It is not a traditional technique but offers a fairly simple way to work. For the two methods of square knotting, one on cord and the other on latch canvas, turn to Chapter 8.

This square-knotted circular pad is 16 inches in diameter and required 16 feet of tied cording and 16 feet of untied, or plain, cording. The pantyhose were bleached and then dyed in purples and reds. A 1-inch-thick circle of foam rubber 15 inches in diameter was put on the back of the pad with a 16-inch circle of felt over the foam. The felt was whipstitched to the outside coil of the pad to cover the foam and hold it in place.

A spring bouquet of double flowers on florist's wire.

Spring Bouquet

A bud vase holds a small bouquet of shimmering, gossamer flowers of dyed nylon on florist's wire. These double flowers, 2½ to 4 inches wide, were made by Patt Rank. For directions for making such flowers turn to Chapter 7.

Woven Rug

A traditional floor loom, warped with heavy cotton thread, was used to make the striped rug. Marge Barr wove this using nylon stock-

Loom-woven rug of varied beige tones of nylon stockings is 33 inches by 60 inches.

ing strips cut into spirals one inch wide. It is indicative of the durability of the material to know that the weaving was completed more than forty years ago! At that time, stockings were not seamless, so the slubbed texture in the weave is created by the seams in the stockings. It is ideal for the swimmer who needs a quick-drying pad for sunbathing.

Wreath-Framed Mirror

Abundant fruits and flowers frame this mirror. The extravagantly plump fruits, rosettes, and leaves are formed of stuffed mesh hose, predyed in summer colors.

Fruits are made by gathering small circles of nylon and stuffing them with batting. The leaves were formed on cardboard shapes fol-

Colorful, plump fruits, rosettes, and leaves wreath this mirror.

Clothes hanger padded with nylon square knots.

lowing the directions in Chapter 6. The rosettes are made according to the directions given in Chapter 7. The abundant harvest is then stitched and glued to a nylon-covered base to which a mirror was first secured.

Padded Hanger

A padded clothes hanger can be made by covering a wooden hanger with knotted stocking strips. It provides a secure surface for a smooth fabric or for an open-neck dress or blouse.

Starting with the toe end of the leg, tie a firm square knot over the hanger. Cut the stocking off about 1/2 of an inch from the knot and repeat. When you have used the leg from the toe to the mid-calf section and it has become too bulky, cut the remaining length into two equal strips. Continue the tying with the new strips until the hanger is covered. Using brightly dyed hose makes even the closet look festive.

Baker's Wife, a skirted stocking figure, conceals a bank. By Margaret Trembley. (Photos by Jim Walsh)

Baker's Wife Bank

The Baker's Wife bank holds more small change under her apron than you might expect. The Baker's Wife is constructed over a glass apothecary jar which serves as an armature for the soft stuffed figure. The top is made like the stuffed figures in Chapter 6. The figure is tied to the lid of the jar but not glued. The skirt is tied around the neck of the jar.

The Baker's Wife's plumpness could conceal treasures of any kind —even jewelry. She also can act as a cookie jar, since the top figure and the skirt can be removed to wash the jar, and an apothecary jar is airtight.

Square-Knotted and Felt Rug

The rug is 22 inches by 36 inches and combines bands of square knotting and strips of felt machine-stitched to latch canvas. See

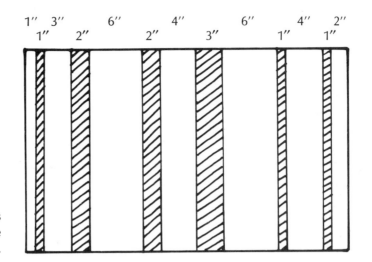

| 1″ | 3″ | | 6″ | | 4″ | | 6″ | | 4″ | 2″ |
| 1″ | | 2″ | | 2″ | | 3″ | | 1″ | | 1″ |

The shaded areas are knotted nylon, the plain areas are felt.

Chapter 8 for instructions in square knotting. The felt strips were cut 3 inches longer than the width of the rug and were machine-sewn to the backing. The extra 1½ inches of felt on each end were turned under the canvas as a hem. It is not essential to use felt, however; other

Bands of felt and square-knotted nylon make this rug.

fabrics can be substituted. Wool strips make a heavy durable rug. Any washable fabric, such as upholsterer's-weight cotton, duck, or canvas, can also be used. Raw edges of the fabric strips will be concealed by the nylon fringes. Rugs made with cottons would, of course, be machine washable.

The hose used in this rug were bleached and dyed to blend with the blues and greens of the felt bands.

Coil Basket

Pantyhose and fabric strips cover the core material in Peggy Moulton's coil basket made with the lazy-squaw stitch. The patterned fabric combines with the plain-colored pantyhose to add decoration and interest to the basket. Fabric strips were cut ½ of an inch wide and the pantyhose was cut 1 inch wide. A safety pin at the end of the strip takes the place of a needle for stitching between each coil.

Coil basket combines printed fabric with pantyhose strips dyed orange, red, and blue.

Mouse Box

Kay Aronson's Mouse Box is made with 8-inch squares of dyed pantyhose tops. The top and bottom sections of the box are each made with one of these squares along with a square of Dacron batting and another square of pantyhose. The three layers are stacked and stitched together. On top of this, on the lid, is a strip of lighter-colored pantyhose leg section. The bubbles are puffs of batting encased in a square of the leg section and hand sewn to the surface. Hand embroidery and free machine embroidery hold all layers together and stiffen the square. More batting is laid on the inside of the top and bottom squares, covered with a patterned fabric square, and then tufted.

The Mouse Box is an intriguing combination of pantyhose, Dacron-filled nylons, and machine and hand embroidery. 8 inches square, 4 inches high.

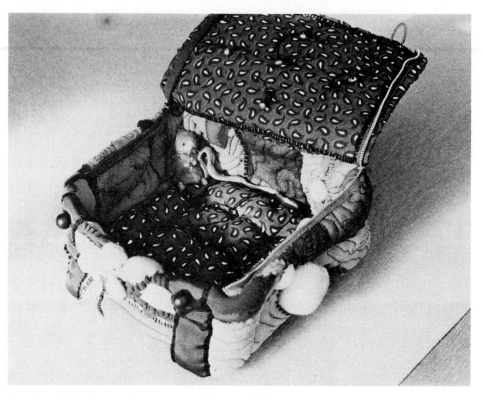

Interior of the Mouse Box.

The four sides are 8-inch squares embellished like the lid and folded in half to make 4-inch-by-8-inch sides. A zipper on each side of the lid closes the box and keeps it secure. There is a very warm and comfortable feeling about the box as evidenced by the handmade mouse that has found a home in an inside corner.

Braided Chair Pad

The stockings used in the chair pad, which makes an equally fine place mat, were dyed in a one-color dye bath over their natural color—the result being varying shades of red orange. The pad is 15 inches in diameter and could easily be enlarged to rug size with the addition of more braiding to the outer edge. For directions, see the section on braiding in Chapter 8.

This chair pad uses the same braiding techniques as a rug.

Coasters and Pot Holders

Hobby shops have for many years carried the small looms for weaving loops of nylon fabric into 5-inch squares. These looms are often sold as children's learning toys or in toy departments. Instead of buying packages of nylon loops, make your own by cutting one-inch-wide strips across mesh hose. For bright colors, bleach and dye the hose first. The loom comes with easy-to-understand directions for weaving and finishing the squares. These woven squares can be assembled to make larger projects, such as afghans.

Coasters catch the condensed moisture
from a cold drink, and dry amazingly fast.

A pot holder made with dyed
stockings in light and dark colors
woven to create a plaid.

Screen of stretched nylons fills a window.

Sheer Window Curtain

An easy but effective method of achieving a sheer window covering is shown in this photograph. Nylon-mesh stockings are tacked to the top crosspiece of the window sash. Each stocking is then stretched across the glass panes and tacked to the bottom crosspiece. Trim away the toes and the excess stocking ends and cover the cut ends with a narrow strip of wood nailed to the frame.

Topiary Rose Tree

This topiary tree uses approximately one and a half dozen roses. A 6-inch Styrofoam ball holds the arrangement. Florist's pins or cor-

The topiary tree shows off
a wide range of colored roses.
Each rose is 2 inches to 3 inches.

A satin rose tops a nylon-covered hosiery box
3½ inches wide and 3 inches high.

sage pins attach the flowers to the ball, and tiny leaves finish the arrangement. To make the roses and the leaves see Chapter 7. Use a 12-inch dowel as the stem. One end of the dowel can easily be pushed into the Styrofoam ball. A colorful pot filled with gravel will hold the tree upright.

Hosiery Box with Rose

The bottom half of Doris Hoover's hosiery box and the rose on the lid are of blue satin. Several contrasting colors of pantyhose are gathered around the edge of the lid and pulled together at the top to frame the rose.

Crossover Curtain

This window covering is similar to the preceding one but the legs are attached to a separately made frame, similar to a picture frame. All the hose are tacked to the inside of the wood so that no ends are visible. With a separate frame you can stretch the nylons diagonally as well as vertically. After the nylon is in place, the frame is set into a window opening.

Transparent nylons are stretched and tacked in place in a wooden frame.

Loom-woven place mat, 18 inches by 12 inches.

Woven Place Mat

Marge Barr wove the place mat on a cotton warp in the 1930s when stockings had seams. One-inch-wide strips of nylon, cut spirally, created an interesting slubbed texture from the seams.

Hoop Rug

This hoop rug was made on a 39-inch metal ring purchased at a hobby shop. Alternating bands of light and dark nylons emphasize

The hoop rug creates its own fringe from the warp of nylons.

the circular shape of the rug. Directions for making a hoop rug are in Chapter 8.

Place Mat on Latch Canvas

Two important requisites of place mats are that they wash and dry easily. This mat meets both needs with no trouble. Strips of dyed nylon were cut one inch wide and as long as the finished length of the mat including the fringe plus a little more to allow for the weaving. The strips were woven on latch canvas. Draw an outline with pencil of the finished size of the place mat on the canvas and then cut the canvas ½ of an inch outside the line.

Weave the strips in and out of the canvas holes the length of the canvas and inside the drawn line. Leave a 1-inch to 2-inch fringe at each end. When all the canvas is filled with the strips, fold under the outside edge of the canvas and machine-stitch through the weaving ¼ of an inch from the turned sides and ends.

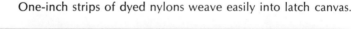

One-inch strips of dyed nylons weave easily into latch canvas.

A soft, plump patchwork quilt was made of squares of bright reds, pinks, yellows, and lavenders.

Patchwork Quilt

Many projects described in this book use the sheer leg section of nylon stockings and pantyhose. But the heavy-weave tops of pantyhose serve as good stretch-knit fabric squares for special projects, such as this one. By cutting off the waistband and center seams of the pantyhose, you have two unbroken panels of fabric about 8 inches square.

Here the large square pieces of pantyhose were made into a patchwork quilt. They were leftovers from other projects and had been dyed in bright colors. Sew the pieces together as for a patchwork panel.

Hosiery box is embellished with Dacron-filled nylon puffs and embroidery. 4 inches square.

Either leave them as large squares or cut them into small and more intricate shapes and patterns. A glazed Dacron batting was used as a filler and the quilt is tacked onto a cotton fabric. The stretchiness of the pantyhose contributes to the puff of the patch pieces after the top has been machine-quilted along the seam lines. A binding of knit fabric finished the edges.

Embroidered Hosiery Box

Hosiery boxes invite the use of nylon hose for decoration as a clue to their contents. Carole Austin used a velour outside and a brocade inside for her fabric box. An elastic encircling the top edge of the lower half keeps the shape round so that the lid will easily slip over it. One leg, with toe and top cut off, makes the scalloped puffs around the elastic edge, while the top of the box is covered with a stocking pulled over the edges and gathered at the center. The nylon-covered balls clustered together on the lid are stuffed with Dacron, and embroidered lines finish the decoration.

Rya Rug

This rug is made with uncut rya knots about 1½ inches long. The oval pattern for the canvas was cut from paper folded in quarters. When the length of the rug was determined, a symmetrical curve was drawn at each end. Add one inch to the pattern and machine-sew around the canvas with a zigzag stitch. Start the rya knots going around the outside edge of the latch canvas inside the stitch, and work to the center. All the stockings in this rug were dyed over their natural color to a richly varied range of golds and greens. The size is 20 inches by 30 inches. Directions for making rya rugs are in Chapter 8.

Oval rya rug has uncut knots for a loop pile 1½ inches deep.

A Della Robbia touch for a mirror frame

A collage of hosiery-covered puffs, stitchery, and patches on a box by Kay Aronson

Topiary tree of fantasy-colored roses

Caterpillar is made of nylon-stuffed puffs.

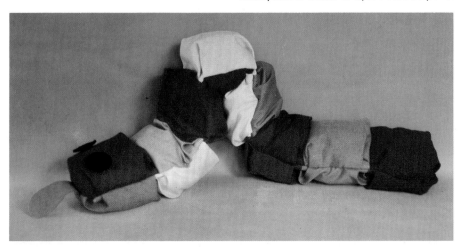

A cat of undyed, sheer stocking

Stitched and clipped nylon gives a
textured surface to this tote.

Crocheted shower rug by Pauline Schwartz

A hoop rug almost finished

Patchwork quilt of the heavier weight tops of pantyhose

Cup dolls

A child's puff quilt

Hamburger pincushion by Lynda Fletcher

Wrapped scuffs

Bird and fish become mobiles when playtime ends.

George Washington
After the Bicentennial.
By June Cooper

Hose stretched on circular frames soften a glass door.
(Photo by Joyce Aiken)

Roses on a sheer hatband

Hopsacking tote with
nylon-wrapped cording
by Patt Rank

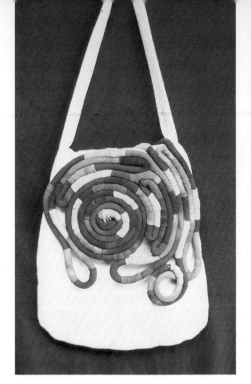

Rainbow babies

Coordinated wrapped cord belt and bracelet by Patt Rank

Spring bouquet by Patt Rank

Spool dolls

Braided place mat

Bas relief faces are fun mirrors.

Square knots on cord cover a foam rubber pillow.

Round latched rug by Sue Mathys. (Photo by Sara Tanner)

Flotsam basket's lid is hinged for easy opening. 3 inches wide and 1¾ inches high.

Flotsam Basket

Coil baskets are made by wrapping a core material of jute or upholsterer's cording with yarn, grasses, raffia, or, in this case, nylon stocking. Marilyn Green's basket is a part of a series called flotsam baskets. She wrapped one-inch strips of pantyhose over jute in a figure-eight stitch. The stocking strips thread easily into a yarn needle for the stitching. All the stockings were left their natural color to fit her flotsam theme. The hinged lid is made of two layers of fabric stuffed with small squares of nylon and decorated with embroidery stitching. The inside bottom of the basket has brown beads sewn to it for a textural surprise when the basket is opened.

The open basket reveals glass beads sewn to the inside bottom of the coils.

Traditional tomato pincushion.

Tomato Pincushion

The tomato-shaped pincushion is made of the heavy section of knit pantyhose and topped with leaves of the lighter-weight legs. To make the pincushion, cut a square from the top of pantyhose dyed red, and put a thin layer of cotton batting in the center. Now take one or two legs and gather them up as if you were going to put them on. Place them on top of the batting and gather the square of pantyhose up around them. Sew or tie together. Clip excess nylon away from tied ends. Cut a circle, 5 inches across, of mesh stockings dyed green, and cut leaf shapes from the outer edge toward the center. Place the leaf section over the gathered section of the ball and hand-sew to conceal the tied top of the tomato.

Shower Rug

Pauline Schwartz crocheted this rug as a fast-drying shower pad. It is 29 inches square and sculptured to keep it from slipping on a wet floor. Cotton rug strips were combined with natural-colored stockings for a change of texture and value. Single and double crochet

This shower rug makes footing secure.

stitches are used throughout. The sculptural effect was achieved by a change of hook size and fabric thickness.

Sachets

For your linen closets or for travel, sachets are quick and easy projects. They make fragrant travel gifts, and are a welcome addition to any suitcase. These sachets are brightly colored sections of nylon stocking. For a lingering scent, wrap batting around dried potpourri.

This sachet is made
from a square of nylon.
The rose-petal and
cinnamon potpourri is
tied up in the nylon
with a ribbon and
artificial flowers.

Or cover a section of stick cologne or small pieces of scented soap with
batting. Slip the ball of batting into the stocking, and tie it at each end
with decorative ribbons. Then cut off the stocking to within 2 inches of
the knot. A straight cut, pulled gently to the sides, will give a rolled
edge. For a feathery edge, clip into a 2-inch fringe.

Sections of nylon stocking, tied at each end, hold pieces of
perfumed soap or fragrant potpourri in cotton batting for the traveler.

Place mat of crocheted hexagons, stitched together to create a zigzag border.

Crocheted Place Mat

Small hexagons crocheted separately were assembled by whipstitching them together. The stitch is single crochet with six double crochet stitches spaced equally around the center circle to form the hexagon shape. The zigzag edges of the place mat are a natural result of the six-sided crochet pattern. The nylons were bleached and dyed before being cut into one-inch strips.

Hamburger Pincushion

The funky and somewhat absurd, but nevertheless very usable, pincushion is Lynda Fletcher's creation. It takes some of the pain out

Hamburger pincushion "to go" is assembled from felt buns with hamburger patty, cheese, lettuce, and onions. "Hold the mustard."

Unlosable key ring by Ruth Law.

of mending and is put together exactly the way you'd assemble the real thing.

Circles, 6 inches in diameter, of gold or beige felt form the crusts of the buns, with circles of the same size of white felt for the bread facings. A few knots would add sesame seeds. The hamburger patty is made of two 6-inch circles of brown felt, stacked and machine-stitched all the way around. The center of one side is then slit so that the circles can be turned, putting the seams to the inside. Stuffing—two nylon stockings cut in narrow strips—is inserted and the slit is closed with slip or overcast stitches.

Repeat the slitting, turning, and stuffing for the buns, slitting the white circle on each. Those three shapes are the only ones stuffed. Layers of cheese (4½-inch square of yellow), onion (4½-inch circle of white), lettuce (irregular shapes in green), and tomato (5-inch red circles) are cut from felt. The ingredients are then stacked and skewered together with a few stitches.

Key Ring

This striped man is chock full o' nylons, and clings to a key tenaciously. Ten inches tall, he is a guarantee that a special key to a cellar or store room will never be lost. Ruth Law recycled him from a T-shirt, gave him new life with old pantyhose, and stitched his fingers so that he is permanently hung up over the key ring.

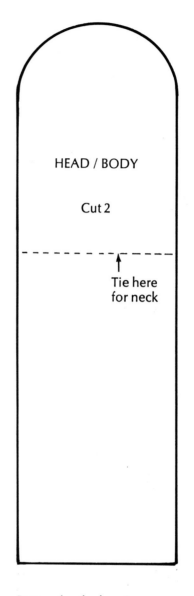

HEAD / BODY

Cut 2

Tie here for neck

Pattern for the key ring. Add seam allowance.

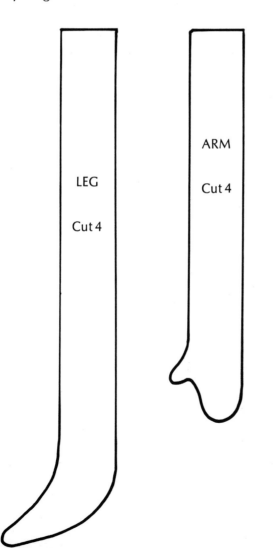

LEG

Cut 4

ARM

Cut 4

Entry Rug

Rows of single crochet with a 2-inch crochet border around the edges were used to make this entry rug. Then diagonal lines of yarn in a double row were stitched on to add color and pattern to the surface of natural-colored stockings.

Plant Hanger

Five nylon hose make a strong and attractive hanger for indoor or outdoor plants. A metal ring, available from hobby shops, fits under the flowerpot rim and supports the pot.

Entry rug made with single crochet stitch is both practical and attractive. This one is 36 inches by 42 inches. By Mrs. Nickerson.

Plant hanger of nylon is strong, durable, and inexpensive to make.

Use five legs and tie each one to the metal ring about 8 inches from the toe end. Bring the toes together and tie them all together in an overhand knot. Twist the upper section of each leg into a tight cord and tie them together in another overhand knot. The tied ends of the toes and tops form a fringe that can be cut into small strips or left whole. The stockings slide to one side to allow the pot to be put into the ring.

This puff quilt
invites any tired toddler
to snuggle up for a rest.
26 inches by 30 inches.

Puff Quilt

The traditional puff quilt or coverlet stuffed with nylon is made by assembling a series of puffs. First select colors and puff size. Next, determine the desired width for the quilt. Join puffs to make the strips going across the quilt (the shorter dimension), then join enough of those strips sideways to make the quilt as long as you want it. Directions for making the puffs for a quilt are given in Chapter 9.

Once the top of the puff quilt has been assembled, a layer of fabric is needed for the backing, which is stitched by machine to the very outside edge of the quilt top and covers the stitching on the back. Raw outside edges can then be bound with strips of matching fabric.

Holders

Nylons can serve as containers for numerous other household items. A cook or gardener with a bountiful crop of onions will find the hose a great help in storing and drying the vegetables. Drop an onion into the toe and tie a knot above it, drop another onion in and knot again. Repeat until the leg is almost full. Leave enough hose at the top

Onions are kept dry
and ready for use.

Travel bag uses the waistband of
stretchy pantyhose for the drawstring channel.
8 inches square.

to tie closed and hang in a garage, cellar, utility room, or kitchen. When an onion is needed for flavoring stew or soup, cut the leg just above a knot and lift out the onion. The others stay in place in the stocking. The air circulating through the mesh and around the onions will keep them free from mold.

Travel Bag

Travel bags made of nylon stockings are so lightweight and require so little space that their presence in a suitcase is barely detected. They expand generously for all the last-minute additions. The bag as well as the colorful patchwork which decorates it is made from the heavier knitted material from the top section of pantyhose. The woven waistband on some pantyhose has an open channel ideal for the drawstring. Cut rectangles or squares from the sides of the pantyhose, eliminating the front and back seams. Add patchwork at the base, then join the side seams, starting just below the drawstring channel to leave an opening for the drawstring.

TIPS

Before pantyhose became a material for contemporary art and soft sculpture, the old stockings were kept for everyday uses. They still serve multiple household needs. The following uses for nylon stockings and pantyhose are not illustrated but are worth mentioning.

SHOE PROTECTORS. Travelers will find mesh stockings make good shoe bags. They have the benefit of being less bulky than store-bought ones and are certainly less expensive.

DECORATING EGGS. A popular method for decorating Easter eggs uses nylon stockings to hold fern leaves or flowers in place while the eggs are dyed. To make one of these lovely eggs, cut a stocking into a 5-inch square and place a small sprig of fern in the center. Put an egg on top of the leaf and gather the nylon tightly around the egg and tie the nylon with a string or rubber band. Then dye as usual, and when finished, gently remove the stocking and leaf. The result will be a natural-looking, delicately decorated egg.

CARRIERS. Budding young naturalists who avidly collect bugs or insects can slip a glass collecting jar into a stocking for easy carrying. If in the excitement of the hunt the jar is dropped and broken, the glass and insects are contained inside the stocking. Any time a child carries a glass or breakable container, a stocking cover will eliminate the danger of broken fragments being scattered.

SPROUT-JAR COVERS. For the health-food enthusiast, home-grown sprouts are a must, alfalfa seeds and mung beans being among the easiest natural foods to grow. Sprout-jar covers are made from the sheer section of a clean stocking. Cut a 6-inch square, place it over the mouth of the jar and secure it to the glass with a canning ring, a piece of string, or a rubber band. The seeds inside will receive the air circulation necessary for growth, while the stocking allows for the everyday rinsing and draining needed for germination.

STRAINER. Painters have been putting nylon stockings to use for years. Stretch the ankle and leg section of a stocking over a tin can— let the toe hang inside the can—and pour old or lumpy paint through the stocking to strain and clear it. If you wish, you can secure the stocking on the can with a string or rubber band before pouring. After straining the paint, the stocking can be lifted off and thrown away. There are plenty more for the next job.

PACKAGE CORD. Rather than search for a piece of string or cord to tie up an important package for mailing, check your stocking bag. You'll find the perfect solution to your needs for a strong, durable cord. Use a whole uncut single stocking and tie it securely around the package. The stretchiness of the stocking helps hold the knots tight. When traveling, keep a snagged stocking for the same purpose. It's perfect for tying around a package too large to put in your suitcase, and it's much easier on your hands to carry than string.

PLANT TIE. A strip of nylon stocking used to support a sprawling house plant is a lot easier on the plant than a piece of string or cord. The stocking has just enough stretch and give so that it does not bruise the plant, yet is strong enough to hold even a large outdoor shrub.

VENT COVERS. For unvented clothes dryers, a stocking leg slipped over and secured to the exhaust vent catches the lint and can be conveniently thrown away when full.

BIRD CARRIER. Some zoos have used pantyhose to transport exotic birds. A bird is slipped into a length of nylon stocking. The hose keeps the bird from flying but does not completely immobilize it. Carried this way the birds can see and breathe normally and seem less likely to panic.

4.
Playthings

The kaleidoscopic versatility of pantyhose astonishes even the most skeptical among us. We are now going to put to use its suitability for making toys and playthings. Many of the playthings shown in this chapter are made for children; some are made *by* children. All are charming, inviting, easy to make, and inexpensive.

Cat

Pantyhose makes a marvelous covering for soft forms—animals as well as people. The cat is stuffed and stitched using all the approaches used in doing nylon-stocking people figures in Chapter 6.

The nylon selected should be the stretchy, not the shaped, kind, and the stuffing should be Dacron. The toe of the stocking, with the dark reinforcement, makes the ears. Stitch on cheeks and button nose, and cut the eyes from felt. A ribbon at the neck covers the cord that separates the head from the body. Arms and legs, made separately, are stitched to the cat's body, as is the tail.

Bird

Another nylon-covered toy is the bird. Brightly dyed pantyhose were used for the simple stuffed shapes, each of which was made individually and then assembled with the others. The toes of the hose were used for all parts of the bird, making use of the seams at the ends of each stocking. One toe was plumply stuffed, then tied off, for the body. The tied end was later covered with the cone-shaped felt beak, whipstitched into place. A second toe section was stuffed and cut off straight to make the tail. The cut end was whipstitched shut, and the piece was shaped by easing the stuffing into the desired shape. Each of

Toddlers love this stuffed cat with a head made of the toe of a stocking. 6 inches high.

Lavender bird has orange wings, a blue tail, and a beak of yellow felt. 8 inches long with a 6-inch wingspan.

The chubby fish is in shades of blue. 8 inches long.

the wings is made from the toe ends of other legs. The wings, tail, and felt eyes are whipstitched onto the body.

Fish

A fish, suspended by thread, swims effortlessly along. Because it is so lightweight, the fish turns with the slightest breeze. One section of nylon stocking forms the body and the tied end makes the fish's mouth. In the final steps stuffed fins are stitched on. An elastic cord allows the fish to bob up and down.

Jump Rope

Whether for a child's play or an adult's exercise, a lightweight and strong jump rope can be made in minutes with very little effort.

Select two pairs of pantyhose with even mesh weave from waistband to toe, since it is best if the finished braid is of uniform weight

Jump rope of dyed nylons is braided to a comfortable 5½ feet for this young rope skipper.

and is unbroken by added lengths of stocking strips. Each pair of tall-girl pantyhose will give you two of the required three strips of nylon 7 feet long. The stocking stretches as it is pulled and braided, so a 7-foot length of hose braids into a 7½-foot jump rope, which is long enough for an adult. Children will not need such a long one, so shorter pantyhose will serve well.

Cut each pantyhose top and leg into one long continuous strip with the toe seam at the middle of the length. To do that, make one cut straight down the outside of the leg section starting at the waist and going to the outside toe seam. Now cut approximately 4 inches away from the first cut on the front of the pantyhose. Start at the waistband and continue straight down the inside of the leg section to the inside toe seam. Cut the back of the pantyhose the same as the front and you should have one long length of nylon with which to braid as in the drawing. Repeat for the other leg of the same pair and on one leg of the second pair.

After you have cut three long lengths of hose, match and tie the three ends together in one knot about 4 inches from the end, leaving a tassle. Braid the length of the stocking strips, keeping a firm tension, to within 5 inches of the ends. Now tie the ends together in a single knot. This gives you 4-inch fringes on the ends for handles.

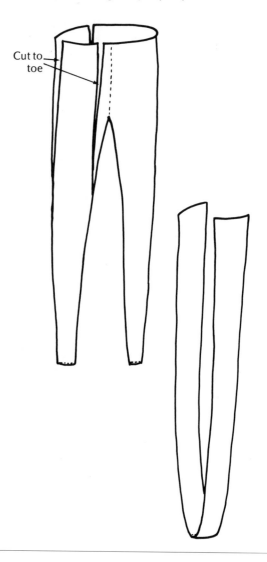

Cutting the legs to form strips for braiding the jump rope

Cut to toe

Five green pea-pod people
peer out when the pod is opened.
(Photo by Karen Jahncke)

Giant Pea Pod

Karen Jahncke's giant yard-long pea pod opens to reveal five residents. The faces, made from transparent green nylons, have an amusing but eerie, unearthly green cast. Their legume missile might have deposited them here from outer space. The faces can be attached to the pod with squares of Velcro so they can be changed around. And for a younger child the size can be reduced. To make the faces see Chapter 6.

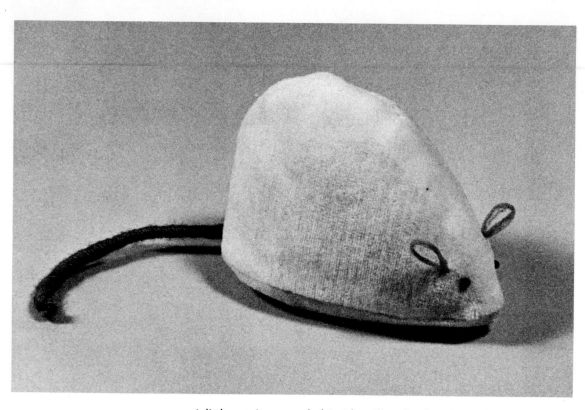

A little catnip concealed inside will make this the perfect toy for a cat lover's cat. 5 inches long.

Mouse

This solemn little mouse is plump on a diet of four whole nylon stockings. Because the velour from which the cuddly creature is made is thick and heavy, no lumpiness from the wadded stockings will be apparent. The mouse is cut according to the pattern. The two side pieces are joined, right sides together, along the curved back with a $\frac{1}{2}$-inch seam. Sew on small, shiny-black beads or buttons for eyes.

Very narrow rings of nylon stocking (cut crosswise on the hose) make the ears. Stretched, the nylon makes a thin, string-like line which can be threaded through the eye of a darning needle. Two loops are sewn for ears, and knotted on the inside. For the tail, use a piece of jute or cording. Join the sides of the mouse to the bottom, right sides facing, using a ½-inch seam. Leave about 2 inches unsewn at the tail end of the mouse. Turn right side out, stuff with four nylons, one of which has catnip inside, then whipstitch shut, inserting the tail in place as you sew.

Pattern for the mouse

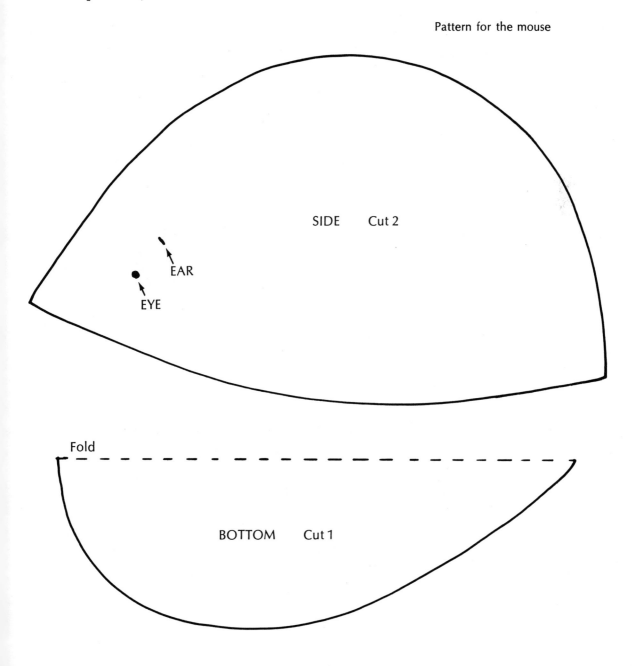

SIDE   Cut 2

EAR

EYE

Fold

BOTTOM   Cut 1

Jack and Jill in Boxes

Jack and Jill in their boxes were made by Yvonne Porcella. The bodies are of brightly colored cotton material and the faces are panty-hose stuffed with Dacron batting as described in Chapter 6. They both have yarn hair. Yvonne made the boxes of yarn using pin-warp weaving with knotless-netting details on the lids. A soft, sculptured carrot closes the Jack's box.

Jack-in-the-box pops his head out of a yarn box. Jill-in-the-box has her head attached to the box lid, ensuring that she will always pop up in greeting. 8 inches, open, 3½ inches square, closed.

Spool Dolls

Two spools, stacked one on the other, form a sturdy base for these little dolls. Use white glue to join the spools. Then stuff a head, as

Heads of stuffed nylon hose are tied atop stacked thread spools.

Attaching the head to the spools

shown in the drawing, and pull it over the spool. Tape or tie—or both —as shown, so that the head is secure. Stitch a nose as described for stuffed-nylon-stocking heads in Chapter 6. Add French-knot eyes and a long stitch for the mouth. Hair can be made of yarn, nylon stocking, or unspun wool. Make arms as in the drawing either of nylon (which matches the face) or of dress fabric. Dress the doll with a simple wrap-around dress and a ribbon belt, then add the arms.

Making the arms

Rainbow Babies

The most brightly dyed nylon stockings are used in this collection of charming little dolls. Their construction is basically the same as that used for the spool dolls. Anywhere from one to three spools are used to give varying heights. Stitch the features first, then add the clothing which consists of narrow tubular sections of hose pulled onto

Rainbow babies come in different sizes and colors. 2 inches to 6½ inches high.

the spools and tied in place. Any one of these dolls can be made in a matter of fifteen minutes, and children love watching them come speedily to life as you work.

Rabbit

This big-eared little rabbit is made from a cotton baby sock, size 3 or 3½. Sally Paul made him by first turning the sock inside out and slitting it from the tip of the toe to about 1½ inches from the heel.

Nylon-stuffed
baby-sock critter is
6 inches high.

Slit

TOE

Making the rabbit's ears
and eye sockets

This divides the toe into the two sections that make the ears. Then she
made small darts in the heel, as shown in the drawing. The ears were
machine-stitched and the sock turned right side out and stuffed with
narrow strips of light-colored nylon. After stuffing, tie each ear close
to the head. Squeeze the bridge of the nose and hand-stitch from dart
point to dart point, making eye sockets. Sew from each eye to the center
of the mouth, shaping the cheeks, as shown in Chapter 6. Add felt
teeth, bead eyes, and thread whiskers. Add more stuffing if needed,
and slip-stitch the end of the sock closed. Add a ribbon or bow, and a
tail of ball fringe or yarn.

Halloween Witch

A Halloween witch to decorate a holiday table will delight adults as well as children. Make the stocking head according to directions in Chapter 6. Then pull it over the base of a Styrofoam cup. The hair is coarse yarn and the clothes are made of felt and glued to the cup. A pine-needle broom has a stick for a handle and is sewn to the witch's sleeve.

The Halloween witch is 6 inches high. By Lynette Cedarquist.

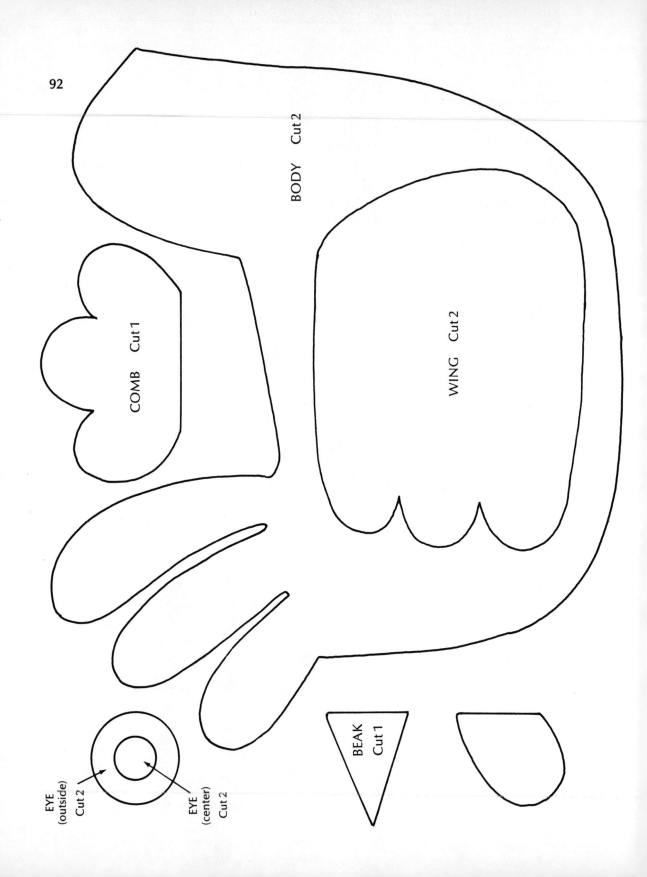

BODY   Cut 2

WING   Cut 2

COMB   Cut 1

EYE (outside) Cut 2

EYE (center) Cut 2

BEAK Cut 1

Setting hen is of deep pink felt with orange wings.

Setting Hen

The relaxed chicken is cut from felt, according to the pattern. For stuffing, nylon legs are cut lengthwise into four strips each. First the eye pieces and wing of the hen are sewn to the front piece. Beak and comb are pinned into place. Then front and back are joined by stitching at the outside edge. This one was sewn by hand using a running stitch, though machine stitching would work as well. When the sewing is completed about two-thirds of the way around, stop stitching and slip the stuffing into place. Then continue sewing. Animals can be as lightly or tightly stuffed as desired. Because felt is not truly washable, toys made from it cannot be run through the washer without some shrinkage.

Pattern for the setting hen

Nylon stocking and batting makes a doll's head on a clothespin base.

Forming the head
on the clothespin

Clothespin Doll

The old-fashioned doll suggests that recycling stockings is not new. The beribboned girl, found in a thrift shop, is made over a clothespin base. Batting is wrapped around the head of the clothespin and then a piece of stocking is slipped over that as in the drawing. The stocking is tied in place just below the ridge in the clothespin. Arms are made from thin rolls of stuffed stocking tied at the end to form a ball for a hand. Her costume includes petticoat and pantaloons, and the face is detailed in embroidery.

Making the arms in the sleeves

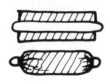

Adding the dress

Hammock

Not one, but two recyclable materials are used to make the hammock. Plastic ring carriers from six-packs of soft drinks combine with twisted nylon stockings for an inexpensive and easy-to-make project. The finished hammock is very elastic and bouncy and makes a marvelous summer entertainment. To assemble your own, follow these directions.

Using square knots, tie pantyhose legs together end to end until you have a 6-foot length. Eighteen of the 6-foot lengths of tied hose will be required to make a hammock the size shown in the photograph.

Plastic soft-drink carriers and nylon hose combine to make a flexible hammock.

Close-up photograph shows how carriers are woven in.

On the floor or a large table, lay out plastic rings in a single row 5½ feet long, placing them so that the 3-circle sides are touching. This will be the finished length of the hammock, though when you get into it, it will stretch much longer.

Then lay another row of plastic rings over the first, staggering them so that each new set of six rings overlaps halfway onto each of two separate carriers in the first row. When all the carriers are laid out in the first row, there will be a double layer of plastic rings.

Take two of the 6-foot lengths of stocking and tie one end of each to a 3-inch metal ring. Twist the stockings together to make a rope. Now weave the end of the rope not tied to the ring in and out of the first, or outside, line of circles in the plastic ring carriers, and tie the twisted stocking rope to another 3-inch ring at the opposite end from the first. Repeat for the middle line of circles.

Before weaving the third line of circles, lay out another row of plastic carriers (the same number as in the first row). Overlap them over the third line of circles of the first row set down. Weave a twisted rope of stockings through this row. Continue overlapping plastic carriers and weaving with twisted stocking rope until you have woven nine ropes through the plastic.

Tie a piece of strong rope through the 3-inch rings at each end of the hammock and attach to two trees, about five feet above ground. Pull the hammock out flat and taut when you tie it to the trees. The nylon-stocking rope stretches when you get into the hammock, so unless it is tied high off the ground it will sink too low to swing in it. Because of the flexibility of the carriers and the nylon, the hammock tends to mold around the body.

Country Mouse

The wide-eyed Country Mouse can easily be made by a child. A wire coat hanger is first bent as shown in the drawing. A stretchy or mesh nylon stocking is then pulled over the wire frame so that the stock-

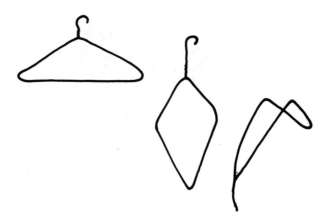

Construction for wire clothes-hanger animal heads

ing toe is at the pointed end. The reinforced part of the stocking toe is then tied off so that the knot becomes the nose. Glue paper eyes and ears to the face using a fabric glue or paste. Add pipe-cleaner whiskers.

Brown nylon stretched over a coat-hanger frame produces a country mouse in minutes.

The mouse can be used as a very simple puppet. Most children simply enjoy marching around with the animals. Bend the hook end of the hanger closed to make a safer, more comfortable handle to grasp. With a table serving as the stage, the puppeteer can sit behind the table, concealed by a cloth.

Doe

The young doe is the creation of a six-year-old. The toe of a stocking is drawn over the bent wire so that it fits snugly. The opposite end is tied off with a cord next to the hook. Eyes, shiny ears—the better to hear you with—and a little nose, all of paper, complete the features.

Dragon

To make the dragon's snapping jaws, you need two wire hangers. Each is stocking covered, with the toe sitting smoothly at the end. Yellow-paper teeth line the open mouth, and the beast spots his victims

The dragon snaps
viciously with
paper incisors.

with Styrofoam-ball eyes. For the dragon, the hook should be straightened out and taped so there will be no sharp points. The two separate wires of the head are taped together at the handle ends. Otherwise his mouth falls slack and the powerful jaws unhinge!

Horse

This horse is made by the same method as the other coat-hanger animals. A mane of fringed nylon, glued in place, flops gently as he canters along. Eyes and ears are paper. If you straighten out the hook to form a handle, tape the sharp ends.

Horse has a reinforced toe for his mouth
and a mane of nylon fringe.

Three dolls snuggle under a patchwork of bright woven squares.

Doll Blanket

Nylon-stocking loops are woven into squares on a small, simple loom. These were made on one of the children's looms that weave 5-inch squares with nylon loops. Make your own loops by cutting 1-inch-wide strips across dyed mesh hose. Here the squares are joined at the edges by slipping one loop inside the next until you reach the edge of the blanket. The last loop is then tack-stitched into place. A line of straight machine stitching secures the outer edge of the blanket so that those loops can be left as a fringe.

Caterpillar

Children delight in colorful playthings made from puffs. For this caterpillar, nylon-filled puffs are joined into two strips, each containing eight single puffs. The two strips are then joined, placing right sides

Caterpillar of red, yellow, and pink puffs is a voracious consumer of the pantyhose
with which he is stuffed. 25 inches long.

together and stitching along one long edge and both ends. The puffs
are folded back, wrong sides facing, and the open side is slip-stitched
shut. The felt eyes and tongue, cut according to the pattern, are hand-
stitched or glued into place. To attach the tongue more firmly, you can
insert it into the end seam when joining the strips.

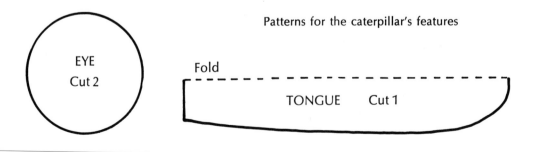

Patterns for the caterpillar's features

EYE
Cut 2

Fold

TONGUE   Cut 1

Since they are very lightweight, even the smallest child can grasp these toys and carry them about, and they can be tossed into the washing machine for easy cleaning. Serpents and dragons of all sizes provide hours of fun for toddlers. Directions for making the puffs are in Chapter 9.

Cup Dolls

These little figures seem dignified and aloof, despite their humble underpinnings. Start each with an inverted Styrofoam cup. Make the heads from colored hose, and attach them to the base as shown in

Mysterious, unsmiling little dolls are made on Styrofoam cups.

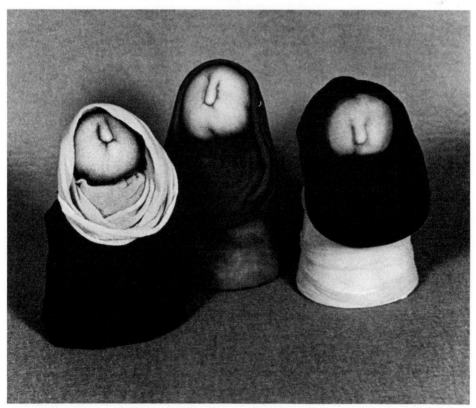

Forming the hood

the first drawing. Select a mesh stocking, trim off the toe, and cut two sections, each 5 or 6 inches long, from the ankle and leg parts. Pull one section over the head and onto the cup. Tie around the neck, with three-quarters of the stocking section above the tie, as shown in the second drawing. A second section of hose, in a contrasting color, is pulled up over the bottom of the cup. One raw end of the second section tucks under the bottom of the skirt, inside the cup; the other is folded to the inside and covers the lower raw edge of the top part. The top part is then pulled down to expose the face and form a hood. Stitch a nose as described in Chapter 6, and the doll is finished.

A whole collection of these dolls can be made in thirty minutes. Children spend hours making and playing with the intriguing-looking dolls, and they readily become simple hand puppets. Small children can cram a fist into the Styrofoam cup, then hold it up so that the puppet appears over an improvised stage—the back of a chair or the top of a table.

Puppets

Because stitching nylon-stocking heads gives marvelous characterizations, hand puppets made this way are particularly expressive. The puppet must be made so there is room for one or two fingers to reach inside the head and hold it up and move it. The thumb and one or two other fingers can be used to manipulate the arms, if they are added. An easy way to begin is to use a small cardboard tube. A section from a paper-towel or toilet-paper tube will do. Fit the tube over the two fingers to determine the appropriate height. If it is too long, cut enough off to get the desired length, if it is too large, find a smaller tube or add stuffing to the inside until it fits.

Next, wrap batting around the outside of the tube and draw a nylon stocking, knotted to close one end and with the knot turned to the inside, over the batting. Be sure that some of the batting spreads all the way down the outside of the tube to cover it. Tie off an area to suggest the head, making sure that the cord goes over some of the batting as in the drawing. Then make the stitched features as explained in Chapter 6. Stitches cannot go through the tube, but to get depressed areas, the stitches can be drawn to one side and then to the back. When the head is finished, fabric clothes can be added by sewing them directly to the cord at the neckline. If sleeves are sewn

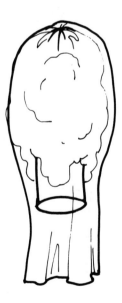

Putting the head on the tube

and left open, the puppeteer's fingers can be slipped through. The ends of the puppeteer's fingers then suggest the hands of the puppet. To make a large hand puppet, give the puppet a long garment, covering the puppeteer's arm as far down as the elbow.

The Little Red Riding Hood is made this way. Hands made of stuffed hose are added, yarn hair is sewn into place, the nose is shaped as shown in Chapter 6, and the features embroidered.

The Pinocchio puppet is made of stuffed nylon stocking. Two fingers hold the tube (over which the head is formed) upright. Thumb and third finger manipulate the arms. A cardboard tube from bathroom tissue was used as the base. A smaller tube of cardboard was attached with masking tape to the larger one as a base for the nose. Since

Stuffed-stocking head is tied over a cardboard tube to make a Little Red Riding Hood puppet. 7 inches high.

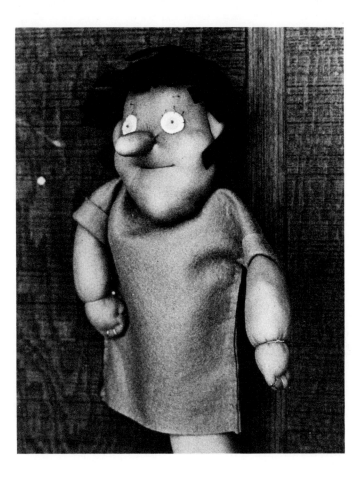

Pinocchio puppet has an
orange dyed-nylon face and arms
and a mustard-color felt shirt
to cover the puppeteer's hand.
12 inches high.

it is the nature of nylon hose to draw back to its original shape, the smaller tube ensures that Pinocchio's nose will remain long. Padding, then nylon hose, were added to the tubes, and the nose was tied at the base to exaggerate its shape. The arms are stuffed hose.

5.
The Gallery

Projects that don't fall neatly into compartments or categories have been collected in this section—a kind of gallimaufry or hodgepodge of miscellany. Quite a few of these projects use the techniques described in Chapter 6 on doll making, soft sculpture, and faces. Many of them are essentially nonfunctional creations, some are done tongue-in-cheek, and others are truly gallery pieces.

The Trophy

The hunt is splendidly burlesqued in this soft sculpture by Susan Morrison. The smug satisfaction and glowing pride of the huntress, after snaring her quarry, is captured perfectly in the stitched nylon-stocking face.

Harvest Messenger

The delightful winged figure is suspended by a cord. She carries a greeting, inscribed on a scroll, along with a delicate bouquet of dried flowers and seeds. The stitching on the stuffed-nylon-stocking head is

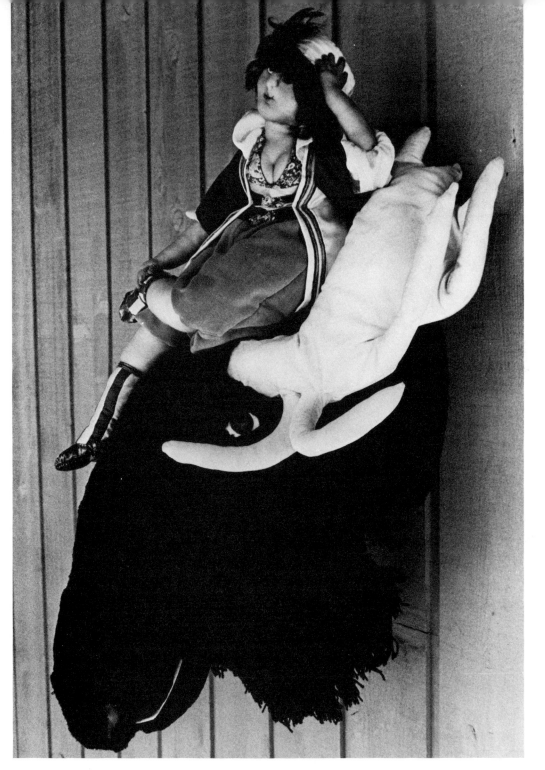

This fine spoof is 36 inches from the tip of the animal's nose
to the top of the huntress's head.

Harvest Messenger by Susan Morrison.

kept simple under a hairdo of yarn. Wings are stuffed, as are the arms and the body. A crisp organdy apron edged in lace covers the skirt.

"Mirror, Mirror, on the Wall . . ."

The mirror frame offers thirteen ravishing beauties—some of them can claim only "inner" beauty. They surround your own reflection like handmaidens. Designer Karen Jahncke made their fabulous hairdos of camel hair, mohair, yarn, and fake fur. She used an oval dime-store mirror and epoxied the finished heads to the glass.

Some of the encircling faces make looking into the mirror a pleasure! 19 inches by 26 inches. (Photo by Karen Jahncke)

Portrait Mirror

Martha T. Frey created this piece with nylon stretched over a padded, flat base as in Chapter 6. The delicate bas relief was achieved

Portrait Mirror
set into an 18-inch frame
(Photo by Martha T. Frey)

with stitching and finely embroidered features, such as the satin-stitched mouth, and irises of the eyes, and the wispy bangs.

Tunic

Perhaps because parties are expected to be entertaining, this party dress is exactly that. The tunic top, made of chamois-like fabric that is somewhat stretchy, lends itself to stuffing in a manner similar to that of the stuffed-stocking faces. Nylon-stocking faces were inserted in slits cut into the tunic. The faces are only lightly stuffed so that they tend to flatten as they are sewn.

Detail of the tunic
showing the
stuffed-nylon faces.

The photograph shows the way in which the tunic material allows the nylon faces to peer through. Each face is finished, complete with hair, embroidered features, and artificial eyelashes, before it is set in place on the tunic top. The heads are then stitched to the tunic fabric to hold each in place. A full gathering of material is needed to provide enough fullness to enclose the faces. Lining helps reinforce the back of the set-in faces.

The creator of the tunic wore it to only one regular function, an art-show opening, and found it disconcerting. Everyone stared and

Louise appears reluctant to be recognized, but Ursula is obviously eager to mingle.

smiled and laughed at the faces, but even old friends would walk by without ever getting past the faces to notice who was wearing the dress. Its social life is now limited primarily to functions such as stitchery-guild fashion shows, where one can be assured of a responsive audience!

Name Tags

For a marvelous icebreaker at a meeting or conference, have participants make their own stuffed faces as self-portraits—the construction takes a matter of minutes—or have the hosting group make up the faces ahead of time and pass them out without regard for likeness. Either way, their humorous expressions assure you that *no* one can refrain from smiling. For a dinner party of your own, try doing portraits of your guests and have them seat themselves by identifying their nylon counterparts.

Gigantic Flower

The enormous and glorious flower is made with mesh hose stretched over wire coat hangers. This flower-making method offers a marvelous opportunity to make imposing centerpieces. Any hospitality

A gigantic flower of mesh hose grows over a coat-hanger base.

or luncheon-committee chairman will enjoy their splendid effect on large tables.

First, a coat hanger is bent into a petal shape. The foot is cut off the stocking and the remaining leg section slipped over the wire. Fabric glue is applied to both sides of the curved end of the wire petal away from the center of the flower and the cut end of the stocking is pressed onto it. When the glue is dry, the excess nylon around the glued part is cut away. At the opposite end, tie the stocking and trim excess. The nylon will fit snugly over the center portion of the petal. Since this makes a double layer of stocking you have the option of cutting one side partially away to form patterns within the petals. If you do this, be sure to glue all edges of the petal to the wire before cutting. Circles can be cut into one of the layers to produce two different shades of color. If any of the stocking separates from the wire during cutting, retouch with glue.

The back of the flower, showing the wire stems that have been taped together, then covered with green nylon.

When trimming is finished, bend the petals as desired and arrange four to six in a circle. Add a stuffed stocking ball in the center, made by pulling stocking over a ball of batting. Hold the wire ends of the petals and loose stocking under the center ball together and secure with masking tape. If flowers are to stand up, slip a dowel in among the wires, then tape all stems and the dowel together. When they are secure, cover with florist's tape or with diagonally cut strips of nylon hose dyed green.

Wreath Mirror

Voluptuous nudes gambol and frolic on this mirror frame in a droll parody of a Della Robbia wreath. Using the method described in Chapter 6, the figures are shaped over cardboard and then assembled amid the season's yield of fruits and flowers. Ready-made mirrors, available at dime stores or department stores will provide the easiest form on which to work. For special shapes, unframed mirrors can be attached to solid ovals of plywood or illustration board, leaving a border for the stuffed shapes. Or the centers can be cut out of wood circles or ovals, leaving a frame to be wrapped and decorated. The frame is then set over a mirror.

Spritely nudes, a wee bit past their prime, lounge somewhat wantonly amid fruits and flowers. The frame is 14 inches across.

An animated conversation at the party.

On the other side of the skirt, the men cluster around a girl of obvious charms and generous proportions.

Cocktail Skirt

Cindy Hickok has made a cocktail skirt which itself depicts a cocktail party. The skirt is made from a polyester fabric similar to duck in both weight and body. A ¼-inch layer of foam rubber is sewn to the inside, with lines of machine stitches. These meandering lines define the area of the figures. The entire skirt is then lined.

The nylon-stocking faces, filled with Dacron batting, are machine-stitched to the skirt. Features and details are hand-stitched and embroidered. The women, sprouting hairdos of nylon hose and yarn, chatter away animatedly. Machine stitching outlines their gesticulating hands and the tightly clasped cocktail glasses. Cindy insists that it is *fun* to wear.

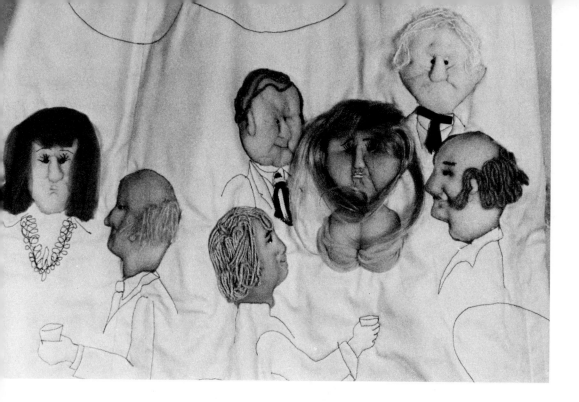

"If the Shoe Fits . . ."

Barbara Threefoot is keen on making stuffed-nylon-stocking heads, but her enthusiasm flags a bit when it comes to bodies and legs. She has therefore done a clever series of containers, which eliminate the necessity for making completed bodies.

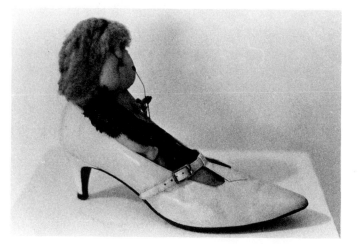

"If the Shoe Fits . . ."
9 inches high.
(Photo by Barbara Threefoot)

George Washington After the Bicentennial.
9 inches high.

Morning-after Mirror.

George Washington After the Bicentennial

The bust of George Washington, made by June Cooper, makes a wry comment on how the Father of His Country might have responded to all the bicentennial celebrating. The bust is mounted for display on a cardboard tube about 3 inches in diameter. The head is not attached to the tube, it merely rests on it.

Morning-after Mirror

A fine mirror for the days when you want a reflection you can bear to look at. Directions for making these mirrors are given in Chapter 6.

Gemini Lady

A collage panel by Ann Gati uses nylons which are stretched, stitched, and draped. Combined with velour, leather, and chiffon, they offer a dramatic textural contrast on this large hanging.

Gemini Lady,
a collage panel, is
33 inches by 54 inches.
(Photo by Fred Ricard)

Shelf Lady

Bigger than life, Margaret Trembley's stuffed-nylon-hose partial figure adds an imposing note.

The Shelf Lady peers coyly over her arms. (Photo by Jim Walsh)

"Love"

Cindy Hickok's tennis-player is an ingenious construction with nylon-hose body and tubular arms and legs. The slip-stitched seams show on the underside of each arm; the clearly defined stitches on the hands suggest fingers.

The sunglasses are made of wire, with lenses made by dipping the

frames in the hobby-store liquid plastic (Whimsey Dip or Fun Film)
used to make artificial flowers. The big tennis shoes (actually the smallest child-size ones made) give the figure enough weight and stability so that it will stand.

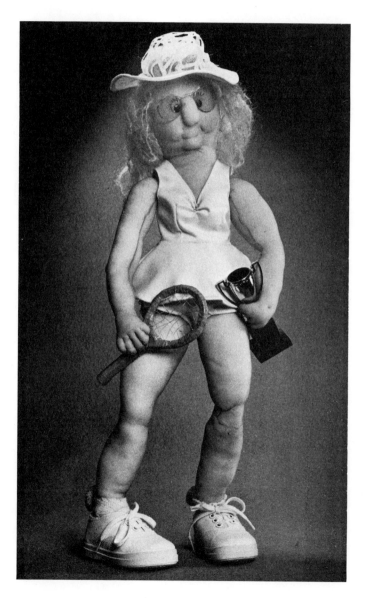

The fully stuffed figure
stands 25 inches high
in sneakers.
(Photo by Gayle Smalley)

"You Stole My Heart Away"
is 12 inches long.

"You Stole My Heart Away"

Susan Morrison's glorious soft sculpture is suspended from a single cord. Made as a valentine, its humorous message and beautifully controlled details would take all the anguish out of getting a run in the newest pair of nylons.

Lady of the House

Pat King's creation caught answering the door is obviously not buying any. Sewn from denim and cotton, the body of the figure is made of two flat pieces of fabric joined at the sides. Feet are made separately and stitched on. The head is given more dimension with a separate panel inserted for the area of nose and chin. The stuffing and stitching create an expression that lets us know she is not about to change her mind. Her crowning glory is her head of pantyhose hair. Strips cut crosswise from the nylons curl into a fashionable coiffure.

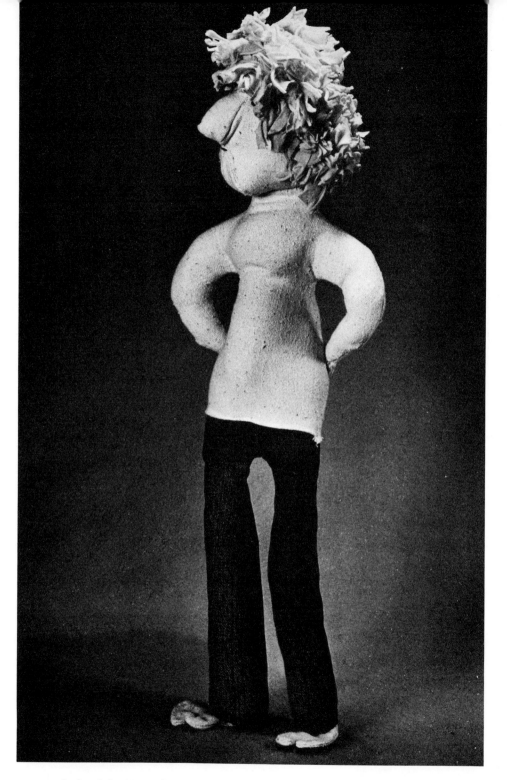

Lady of the House has a no-nonsense approach in her blue jeans and bare feet.
21 inches high. (Photo by Gayle Smalley)

Sister is a good listener
and a steady companion.
(Photo by Jim Walsh)

Sister

Life-size figures are a challenge to construct but they are impressive for the kind of presence they exert. With their mysteriously human qualities, they are extremely difficult to ignore.

Margaret Trembley's Sister, a blonde, buxom companion sporting shapely if somewhat lumpy legs, attracts a lot of attention.

6.

Doll Making, Soft Sculpture, and Faces

Of all the possibilities for salvaging your nylons, few offer greater entertainment value than heads and faces made of stuffed nylon stockings. The process used in making them is simple, the materials are inexpensive, and the results are often disarmingly lifelike.

Stuffed-stocking faces are especially popular with soft-sculpture artists, who find that the material lends itself beautifully to three-dimensional work. Doll making itself has been enhanced by this approach, and many innovative stitchers have used it to add new dimensions to their work.

Try making a few stuffed heads and faces. Then introduce the method to a club, class, or stitchery organization. It will be a most entertaining session. The step-by-step process is simple, with every likelihood of instant success. Once you have mastered it, the stuffed forms can be used in a variety of ways. In this book we have shown puppets, dolls, portraits, jewelry, and clothing projects.

MAKING A STUFFED-NYLON HEAD

The size of a stuffed head is determined by the size of the nylon leg used. For a large head, use the widest portion of the leg near   127 the top, or start with an extra-large size, a Big Mama stocking or pair of pantyhose. Smaller heads can be made from the toe or a narrower portion of the hose.

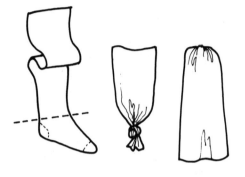

Tying the knot and turning inside out to start the head

Though you will develop variations of your own as you experiment, a good way to start is to cut off the foot of a leg, tying the cut end and leaving the extra length intact for the figure's body as in the drawing. Any kind of hosiery—mesh, knit, sheer—can be used, and each will give a different effect. Colored hose add endless possibilities. Colors will always appear lighter once they are stuffed with Dacron so do not be hesitant about selecting strong colors.

The photograph shows the nylon stocking with the toe cut off and the cut end tied in a knot. To stuff it, slip the stocking over the right

Preparing to draw the cut and knotted end over the ball of batting.

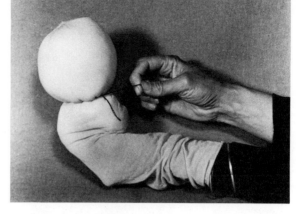

Pulled over the batting, the knot is concealed and the head is tied off.

hand. In the other hand, grasp a smooth ball of Dacron batting. Place the stocking-covered palm of the right hand on the batting and grasp it securely. Then pull the stocking down off the hand and over the ball of stuffing. The knot is now on the inside at the top.

The head must then be tied off. It is important that the cord be tied over some of the batting to help hold the head upright. If the cord is tied under the ball of batting, the head will be very floppy and harder to handle when you work on the face. The batting that extends below the tie also gives you something to hold on to while working the stitches.

To stitch the doll's features, use a double strand of strong or heavy-duty thread and a long needle. Some doll makers prefer a ball-point needle to avoid starting any runs in the nylon, though our experience has been that a long, sharp darning needle is adequate. Occasionally, stockings may run and spoil a face. Stretchy-knit hose seem less likely to run, but there is always some risk. Experience will help you find the most appropriate stockings and needles for your use. When a run does occur, you must be inventive. Sometimes the run can be incorporated into a feature—embroidered into a scar—or perhaps just accepted philosophically like gray hair or freckles and left alone.

The thread color should be related to the stocking color. Use brown thread, for example, on a beige stocking; use red thread on a pink one. The stitches will eventually look like shadows, helping to define the features.

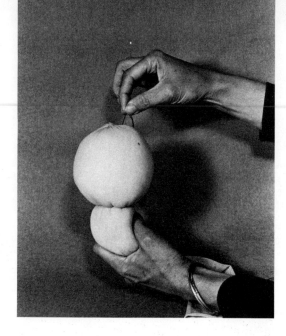

Insert the threaded needle
at top of head near the knot and
bring out on the face area.

The needle is brought through from the top of the head, as shown in the photograph, or from the base at the neckline. If the stitches are brought through directly from the back of the head they tend to flatten the head.

All the shaping on the faces of the stuffed-nylon figures is accomplished in one of two ways—by pinching or by pressing. In pinching, an area is pinched up, and the projecting area secured with back-and-forth stitches. It is used to form noses, eyebrows, chins, or any other bulge or protrusion. In pressing, stitches go from the front or face area to the back. This makes a dent, or a recessed area, and is used for eyes, dimples, and mouths.

The first two or three stitches taken through the batting may not seem to stay in place. Keep sewing, and after five or six stitches have been taken they will begin to hold.

When you start shaping the nose, the back-and-forth stitches will form a line—similar to backstitch—at each side of the nose. To finish the bottom of the nose, pull the thread out at one side and make a large loop down under the nose, then insert the needle at a spot opposite where the thread first came out. Bring the point of the needle

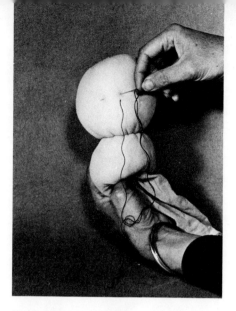

Pinch an area to suggest a nose.

Finishing the bottom of the nose.

out at the very base of the nose. This large loop stitch will shape the end of the nose. To make a more detailed nose, start out with the same loop stitch, but instead of sewing just one stitch, make three. Two of the loops taken at the sides will suggest the nostrils, and the third will form the base of the nose. Once you have mastered the simple loop stitch as a means for sculpting the face, you will find many uses for it, such as making the chin, or forming cheeks. To create a large, bulbous nose, pinch up a big area of batting. Then ease extra batting from inside the head into that pinched section of stocking by using the pointed end of the needle to slide the batting into place.

Another way to make a bulbous or protruding shape is to draw up an area as if gathering. Take stitches back and forth across a circle, with each stitch biting deep into the batting, as shown in the drawing.

Gathering to make a bulbous nose or any kind of bump

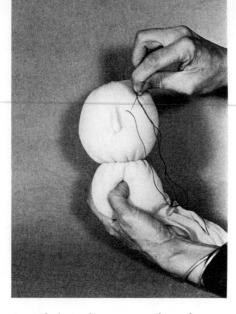

A stitch from the eye area through the head and out the back will make a depression for an eye.

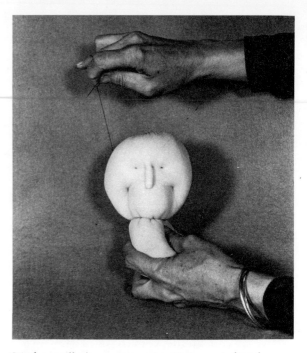

Stitches will also recess areas to suggest dimples.

Then when the thread is pulled tight, the whole area is raised. Wrap the thread around the raised area to hold it tight. The finished round shape can become a buttonlike nose or a witch's warts.

The nose, being central, is a good place to begin the facial arrangement. Since a face is more or less symmetrical, the nose serves as a reference point for other features as they are added. Eyebrows can be formed using the same stitch method as that used for the nose.

Eyes are usually recessed to give them a natural set-in look, in contrast to the pinched areas. The photograph shows the first stitches taken to recess the area for an eye.

The mouth or the ends of the mouth can also be recessed using a similar stitch. Kept small, the stitch will virtually disappear or can later be covered with embroidery. As the mouth stitch is pulled tight, the cheeks puff out and the chin appears. You can also do some of this shaping by using the point of the needle to reach under the nylon to lift and move the batting.

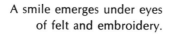

A smile emerges under eyes
of felt and embroidery.

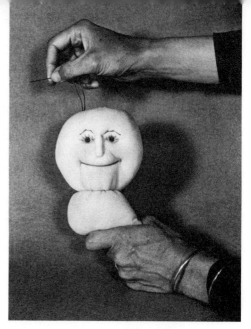

The mouth can be done with a double strand of red embroidery floss. On this particular head the eyes are felt, the lashes and brows embroidery. Any combination of stitching, embroidery, or appliqué will work well. The examples in this book offer a wide range of possibilities.

Dacron batting is an easy-to-use material for making hair. Once shaped to the head, a few tacking stitches in matching white thread will hold the hairdo in place. A hank of yarn also makes a fashionable

Use loose batting for an easy-to-make hairdo.

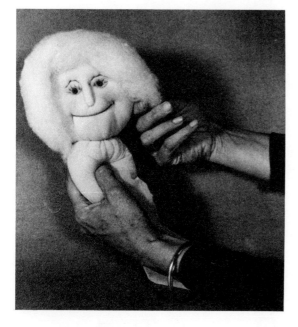

A skein of yarn, tied at one end,
can be tacked into place on the doll's head.

The finished figure is 15 inches high.

coif. Tying the pieces of yarn at either end makes them easier to tack into place. A tie in the center, stitched into place, suggests a part in the hair.

This finished figure has a hairdo of unspun wool. Her arms are made from small tubes of nylon, stitched and then turned right side out for stuffing. Whipstitches over the ends of the arms suggest fingers.

Occasionally, while working on a doll's head, the stitching

through to the back will flatten the head. This results from a combination of too light a stuffing and/or stitches which are drawn too tight. Also, the more stitching that occurs from front to back, the greater the tendency for the head to flatten. Sometimes an additional piece of nylon stocking can be whipstitched to the back of the head, with stuffing inserted as it is sewn in place. That will bring it back to a somewhat spherical shape. It is sometimes possible to simply untie the cord at the neck and add more stuffing.

Flat heads are sometimes needed where faces are to be applied to other articles. Examples in this book appear in the form of pieces on clothing or in novelty jewelry.

COLORING THE FACE

Any coloring added to the face will give an eerily realistic and lifelike touch to the stuffed-stocking faces. Powdered tempera can be used, but cake rouge and eye shadow are easier to handle. A little violet or blue eye shadow, added between eye and eyebrow, makes a tremendous difference in the face. Rouge can be touched lightly to cheeks, chin, and tip of nose. A heavier application can be used to suggest the lips. The powdered makeup should be added after the stitching is complete. Use only a tiny amount to start with, as it is very permanent once it touches the batting, and though a second layer can easily be added, it is difficult to remove any excess. Marking pens, especially the fine-point ones, can be used to draw faces. For painted features, acrylic paints can be applied directly to the stocking. Embroidery, too, adds color to the face. Satin stitches give a smooth, solid area of bright color, and eyelashes can be sewn with one or two strands of embroidery floss.

Artificial eyelashes have a stunning effect; if you select the ones with a sticky backing, their application is greatly simplified. Old wigs offer marvelous doll coiffures, though they must usually be cut into strips or sections and sewn to the head in pieces.

Once you have made several heads you will develop ideas for ways of using them. Some uses have specific requirements. Puppets need an opening for hands or fingers, panels require flattened heads, and three-dimensional figures call for rounded ones. Some projects use faces only; for others, you have to make the entire body.

BODIES, ARMS, AND LEGS

Often, the arms and legs for nylon-stocking dolls are most easily made of fabric. Tubes of fabric can be stuffed and then nylon-stocking hands and feet inserted at the open ends of sleeves or pants legs.

An arm of stuffed nylon, made individually, usually requires a tube-like form which is slip-stitched closed down the back of the arm. To make it, fold a piece of nylon stocking and then machine-stitch it along one side and at one end to make a tubular arm shape. A double row of stitching will make it more secure. The excess material is then trimmed away and the stocking turned right side out and stuffed. The closed end can then be flattened and whipstitched to suggest a hand and fingers as in the first drawing. In place of the whipstitches, backstitches can be used to suggest longer fingers, as in the second drawing.

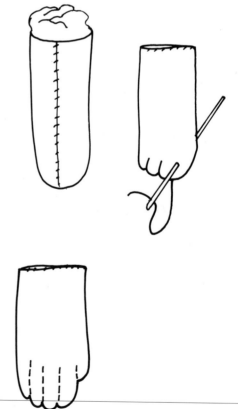

Whipstitching the end of the stuffed tube to form a hand

Backstitching for longer fingers

The body of the nylon-stocking doll can be made in any of several ways. One way is to form it from the part of the stocking that extends below the head. Allow for this when stuffing the head by leaving the length of hose uncut. The body should be well stuffed, then slip-stitched closed at the bottom to the desired size. Arms and legs are then stitched to the body as in the drawing.

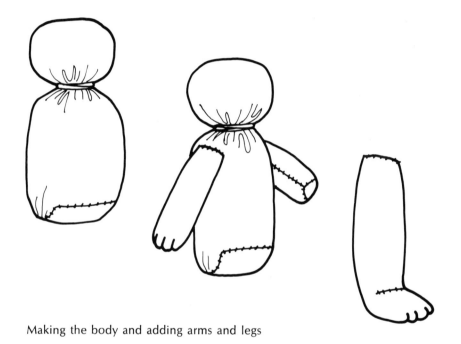

Making the body and adding arms and legs

Sometimes the legs can be made as an extension of the body. The nylon extending beneath the head is first stuffed to make the body. Then the remaining section is split to make the legs. The raw edges of the material are turned under and slip-stitched, and the legs are stuffed as they are sewn. While this seems like a logical way to make the legs, it is usually easier to finish off the body and then add separately made legs. When they are made as a continuation of the body, the legs often end up being somewhat elephantine.

Tennis-ball-can body
for the finished figure

Other ways of making the bodies include using armatures of various kinds. The finished figure with the hair of unspun wool has a tennis-ball-can body. Any can or tube will work; the finished head is attached as shown in the drawing. A tepee-shaped form of cardboard or a heavy yarn cone will also make a good base. Masking tape holds the head securely to the body. Some figures will require a wire armature, or, for a very large and rigid form, a wooden one. The gallery piece "Love," in the preceding chapter, has an armature of copper wire, starting at one foot and running up to the head and back down to the other foot, as shown in the drawing.

The armature for Cindy Hickok's gallery piece, "Love"

CARDBOARD BASES

Where stuffed-stocking faces must remain flat for a specific use, it is easier to make them on a stiff piece of cardboard. The faces in the photograph are made intentionally flat, and can be put to a variety of uses. Several have appeared earlier in the book, as jewelry or as name tags.

To make flat faces, start with a small piece of cardboard cut to the approximate size of the face. Place padding in a mound over the face side, and draw the nylon stocking across the front to the back, where it is stitched and tied. Then sew details onto the face. When stitches must go all the way through to the back, the needle will have to be

Faces formed over
cardboard cutouts.

forced through the cardboard, and may have to be pulled out with a
pair of small pliers.

The reclining figure in the photograph carries the use of cardboard parts one step further. Here, the legs, arms, and body are all
made separately. Cardboards are cut and padded, and nylon stretched
over each. Rows of stitches suggest fingers, and a single stitch makes a
depression for the navel. Breasts are separate little rounds of stuffed

An ample nymph is made by
padding on cardboard.

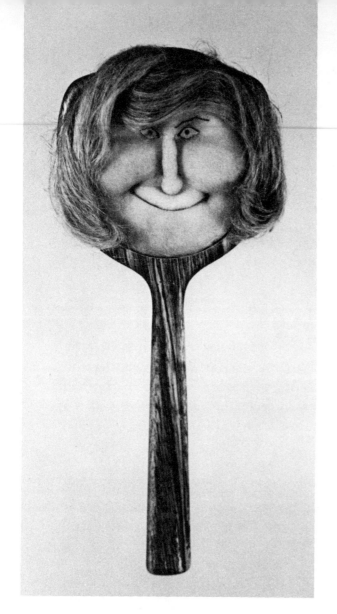

The instant mirror is
12 inches long.

This hand mirror is a stern reminder that
vanity is not considered a virtue.

nylon, slip-stitched into place. Several of these sprightly women are combined in a kind of Della Robbia wreath pattern over a mirror in the Gallery chapter.

The faces on the hand mirrors in both photographs are formed on padded cardboard. In each case, an old broken or distorted hand mirror was used.

If you need to get some or all the glass out of the mirror frame, place it inside a paper bag and twist the bag shut. Then grasp the mirror by the handle and rap it sharply on a counter until all the old mirror falls out. This way, any broken bits of glass will be kept safe inside the paper bag. Most mirrors, though, will come out in a single piece, since the old ones are fairly thick and old glue gives way more easily. If the mirror breaks, shake off the frame carefully and wipe the wood with a damp paper towel to remove any remaining glass. If the handle is to be refinished or repainted, do that before adding the face.

Press a piece of typing paper into the mirror opening to get a pattern of the opening. Cut a cardboard just slightly smaller than the paper pattern so that it will slip easily into place.

Cover the cardboard with batting, mounding it slightly higher at the center, and stretch stocking over it. Stitch or glue the stocking onto the back of the cardboard. Most stitching for the face will be done through the batting only, but stitches can be forced through the cardboard if they must go to the back side. Once the stitching is complete, add powdered color to the face as desired and stitch hair into place, keeping most of the hair on the front side. To attach the face to the mirror frame, apply a layer of glue both to the wood and the back of the nylon head. Let the glue dry partially, then set the face in place.

One such mirror left in your guest bathroom will amuse most of your guests, and only a few will be temporarily startled by what at first appears to be one's own reflection. It is fun to make these as portraits for friends.

7.
Making Flowers

Any cast-off nylon stocking must undergo a complete metamorphosis to emerge as a dainty, ethereal blossom. But given its new life, transparent, soft-colored nylons do form delicate flower petals. Pantyhose, it turns out, have a poetic side!

Varying degrees of density and translucence as well as the color of the nylons affect the overall appearance. Nurses' hose, for instance, provide a full range of whites—opaque, misty, milky, frosted, and silky white. Subtly varying shades of white make an all-white bouquet stunningly beautiful. Mesh hose are more opaque than the smooth, silky kind, and some knits are tighter than others. The tightly knit panty section is denser than the leg sections. While almost any of them can be put to use somewhere, most objects require a particular type for a particular effect.

FLOWERS ON FLORIST'S WIRE

The petal shapes are formed by bending covered florist's wire (available at hobby shops) into loops. To ensure similarity of petal sizes, make each petal by wrapping a wire around a pill bottle, twisting the ends together, and trimming. Brush one side of the wire petal with thick household glue and place it on a piece of colored stocking.

142

Leaf shapes with artificial flower parts can be added to a corsage or bouquet. By Patt Rank.

A double flower and a single flower by Patt Rank.

When the glue has dried, the excess stocking is cut away at the outer edge of the petal. The petal can then be bent and shaped as you wish.

When a number of the petals have been formed and covered, the flower assembly begins. Four or five petals are easy to handle; a double row of petals makes a full, lush blossom. See the photographs for a detail of the flowers. The single-layer flower is made by taking four petals and holding them together at their bases, petals pointing out. Tiny stamens (also purchased at the hobby shop) are placed in the center. All are secured together by wrapping in florist's tape, covering the wires of each petal and joining them into a single stem.

The double-layer flower is made by the same procedure, with the addition of a smaller, second flower inside the larger one.

The leaf detail in the second photograph has a similar gossamer effect but is more simply made in that no gluing or cutting is required. Each leaf shape is formed in wire, the mesh hosiery is pulled over it and tied at the base of the leaf. Tiny artificial flower stamens are placed over the leaf, and it is wrapped with florist's tape. Several leaves are then combined by joining the wrapping.

Tiny rosettes are made by rolling or coiling a folded piece of nylon stocking. Try making one with a strip of stocking cut 2 inches wide and 5 inches long. Fold it in half lengthwise, then roll it up as shown in the drawing. Use thread to tie or stitch it at the bottom to secure the petals in place.

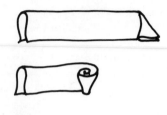

Forming a rosette

A strip of mesh pantyhose, dyed green, can be used to hold them at the base. Florist's wire and tape will also work, though in some projects the base of the flower will not show at all, so the addition of green is unnecessary. As you become accustomed to making the miniature rosettes, you can try smaller sizes, making the strip of fabric both narrower and shorter.

Here the rosettes are tucked into a tiny glass slipper. In other places in this book, rosettes accent a Della Robbia wreath and are also shown in jewelry and accessories. As you work with different sizes and various meshes of stocking you will develop your own preferences as a cultivator as well as a connoisseur of nylon rosettes.

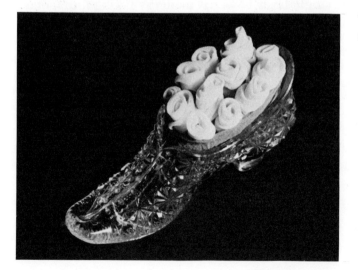

The rosettes in this glass slipper are ½ of an inch across.

Basket holds a Styrofoam ball, packed with nylon roses and tiny leaves.

ROSES

To make a rose, grasp the stocking, or the cut-off leg from panty-hose, at the open end. Gather it the way you would to put the hose on, trying to keep the gathers even. When you reach the toe, the resulting rose will hold its shape. If it does not meet your standards for a qual-ity rose, pull it out and practice some more. When a satisfactory rose is achieved, take a few stitches, going from one side of the rose to the other, trying to catch each gather in the stitches. Keep these stitches near the bottom and do not draw the stitches tight or you will distort the shape of the flower.

Tiny leaves can be added to the roses. These are made from heavy mesh sections of pantyhose. First cut a rectangle from the mesh. Then fold it in half, and machine-stitch a leaf shape on it, leaving one end open for turning, as shown in the drawing. Trim and turn.

Making a leaf for the roses

Open at end for turning

Trim away excess

Separately made petals are stitched together to make a soft, plump flower. By Ginny Rank.

STUFFED PETALS

Another way to make flowers is to use individual stuffed shapes. Each petal in the photograph is a separately tied ball of nylon stocking over stuffing. After tying each ball at the base, flatten out the petal. Sew five such petals together. Finally, slip-stitch another small ball, of a contrasting color, over the tied ends of the petals. The result is a full, three-dimensional daisylike flower.

8.

Rug Techniques

Recycled material has traditionally been used for rug making, and though nylon hose are not one of the traditional materials, they are surely recyclable. Besides being strong, rugs made from pantyhose have the desirable qualities of being soil resistant, durable, and fast drying when made wet—whether by accident or intention. And with dyeing, a full range of gorgeous rug colors is available.

SQUARE KNOT

This is not a traditional method but we found it a simple way to work with pantyhose. You will need 1/2-inch upholsterer's cording as well as pantyhose. Start by cutting 2-inch-wide strips of stockings straight down from leg top to toe. A spiral or diagonal cut will stretch too much when tied. Start at one end of the strip and wrap the stocking around the cording, tying it in a very firm square knot. Cut the two ends off an inch or more above the knot and repeat with the new end of the stocking.

After two or three yards of cording have been covered, start sewing the rug together. Coil the center for a round rug or pad. For an oval rug, follow the instructions given under Braiding. The sewing is done by hand with heavy carpet thread. Work from the back of the

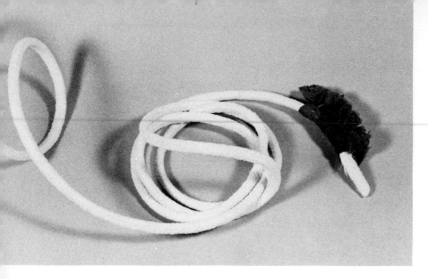

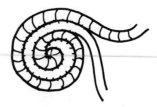

Adding a second, uncovered cord to the coil

Close-up of hose square-knotted over upholsterer's cording.

rug and whipstitch each coil to the preceding one as it wraps around the outside edge.

If the knots are tied very close it may become difficult to sew the covered cording tightly together, and the rug may become too compact. In that case add a second, uncovered cord next to the covered cording as in the drawing, whipstitching them all into a coil. The rug then grows doubly fast and the knots cover the untied cording. If bits of white cording show through on the finished sections of the rug, color them with permanent-color markers. As upholsterer's cording has a soft center it should not be run through a dye bath. Liquid dye colors or thinned acrylic paint can also be brush painted onto the cording before any square knotting is started. A light-colored rug looks fine with tiny bits of white showing through, but for dark colors, the white may be too startling a contrast. The longer the pile, the less chance there is that any cording will peep through.

If you run out of cording before finishing the rug, join a new length by stitching together two angle-cut ends of cording as shown in the drawing. The final knot of the stitching can be kept in place with a spot of fabric glue.

Stitching together two angle cuts of cording

Another method of rug making that uses square knots requires latch canvas, 3½ holes to the inch, as the base for tying the knots. Determine the finished size of the rug and add 2 inches to the width and length measurements for hemming. Cut the latch canvas, then turn the edges under one inch, and machine-sew with a zigzag stitch.

To make the strips, cut the legs off a pair of pantyhose and make long strips approximately 2 inches wide by cutting straight down from the top of the stocking to the toe. The upper portion of the pantyhose is also cut into 2-inch strips after the waistband and center seams are removed.

To tie the strips into the latch backing, first push the end of a strip down through a hole from the front of the canvas. With the other hand, held under the canvas, return the strip to the front of the canvas through an adjacent hole. Pull the strip up through the canvas and tie the ends in a square knot. Space the ties according to the thickness desired.

Felt and square-knotted rug with the knotted strips spilling over onto the felt.

The natural resilience of nylon stocking makes it an ideal material for a latched rug. No amount of sitting, jumping, or rolling around on it will flatten the nylon pile so that one good shake won't fluff it back up.

To make a latch-hook rug, cut a one-inch spiral from the pantyhose or stocking leg starting at the top and continuing down to the toe. This will give you an unbroken strip 27 to 30 feet long. Then cut the strip into working-length pieces for latching, that is, twice the shag height desired plus ½ of an inch (a 2-inch-high pile requires strips 4¼ inches long). For an even-height pile, make a cardboard or wooden guide whose width is one half the length of the working strip. Wrap the long strip around the guide and cut through the strips on one edge, as shown in the drawing.

Cutting even strips
for latching

Latch-hook canvas is available in different widths. Choose the width that lets you use one or possibly both selvages for the sides of the rug. Cut the canvas the correct size plus one extra inch on all cut edges for hemming—unless the edge is selvage; the selvages do not need hemming. When turning cut edges under, match the holes if possible and machine-sew with a zigzag stitch.

A design can be drawn directly onto the top side of the canvas with a permanent marking pen, but make it one with large features. Fine, intricate lines are difficult to retain when latched since the shag falls in all directions.

The technique of latching requires a special hook with a movable latch from which the tool derives its name. The hook is slipped into a hole on the front of the canvas, under a thread of the canvas, and back to the front in an adjacent hole. A strip slides down around the handle and is caught by the hook. As the handle is withdrawn from the can-

Latch-hook rug, showing the design drawn on the latch canvas with a marking pen.
(Photo by Sara Tanner)

vas, the latch closes around the ends and pulls them through the backing to tie a knot. This keeps the pieces securely in the canvas and the tied ends standing upright on the surface.

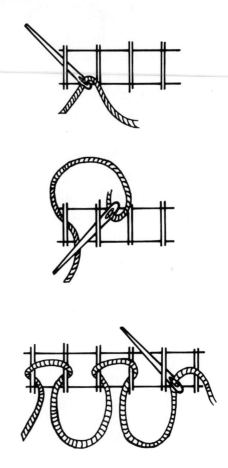

RYA

The technique of rya knotting in rugs creates a cut shag or a loop pile. Yarn is considered the most appropriate material for rya rugs, but old nylons are a successful substitute. Cut each leg into a long spiral one inch wide. Thread a 3-foot strip into a yarn needle and sew into latch canvas as shown in the first drawing. The knots are sewn in rows from left to right and from bottom to top. The length of the pile is determined by the length of the loop between each knot. A shag effect is achieved by cutting the loops after the knotting is complete.

CROCHET

The technique of crochet encourages the use of various materials and is not limited to threads or yarns. Cotton rag rugs have been made this way for years. Now add nylon hose to your list of possible materials. The special advantage of rugs made from nylons is how easily washed and quickly dried they are.

Strips for crocheting can be cut in the same manner as for latch or rya rugs, making a spiral strip of the stocking legs about one inch wide. Make traditional single and double crochet stitches create a sculptural form by changing the hook size and increasing or decreasing stitches.

The nostalgic warmth and comfort of a braided rug comes, in part, from the informality of the multicolor usually associated with this technique. Nylon pantyhose, left undyed, provide a subtle but important change of color in the braid. Unbleached nylons of varying beiges and browns all dyed in one dye bath of a strong color, such as orange, will result in a similarly subtle range of colors.

Hose used for braiding require little preparation or cutting. Dye them if you wish, trimming off the toe and heavy-weave top first. The tubular construction of the hose eliminates the usual need to turn the edges of fabric under before braiding. Machine- or hand-sew three or four lengths of stocking together before starting. The first drawing shows how to join the beginning strands together. Add new lengths as necessary. The braid will be smoother if the addition of new lengths is staggered. After 9 or 10 feet of braid is completed, begin to assemble the rug. Thread a blunt needle with carpet thread or string, and connect the braid by lacing the thread through a loop of one braid and then through the loop of the braid opposite.

A round rug begins with a center coil and the braid encircles it until the desired size is achieved. An oval rug is worked around a straight center line as in the drawing. The final proportion of an oval

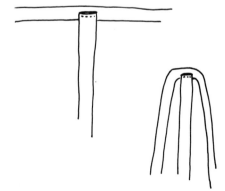

Joining the beginning strands together

Starting a round and an oval braided rug

rug is determined by the length of the straight center braid. To determine how long the straight center braid should be made for the size rug you want, subtract the width measurement from the length measurement, and the difference is the length to make the center braid. If the rug is to be, say 24 inches by 36 inches, subtracting 24 from 36, you get 12, which is the length of the center braid.

Three lengths, each approximately 37 inches long, will braid into a cord 24 inches long. The braid will remain smooth and even if you keep the tension very firm while working.

HOOP

A hoop rug is a variation of the old-fashioned wagon-wheel rug which was originally woven on the metal rim from a wagon wheel. Any similar hoop or ring will work as well.

The hoop is essentially a simple loom of a circular rather than rectangular shape. A reasonable-size hoop for weaving is one that is no wider than the length of the stockings you are going to use. Hobby shops sell many sizes of metal rings sturdy enough for making rugs.

To warp the loom, tie the toe end to one side of the ring. Then take the other end to the opposite side of the ring and tie it to that side. If you tie in four lengths that gives you eight spokes. It will be necessary to add one more spoke since you have to have an odd number of warps to weave in a continuous over-under pattern. The extra strip, which goes only to the center, can be tacked into place with an overcast stitch or it can be tied in, as shown in the drawing. The spokes can be moved around the metal ring to distribute them evenly.

Adding the ninth spoke to the warp

Now the weaving can begin. Use a full leg with just the heavy-weave top cut off. The toe end can be tucked behind and under the

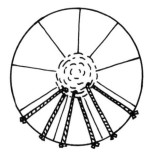

Unfinished hoop rug.
The over-under weave moves from
the center toward the hoop.

Adding new spokes as the
weaving continues

center spokes. Start at the center and weave in and out of the spokes in a circular direction. As you come to the end of each leg push it to the back of the rug and add a new length. The ends are left on the back and can be tied or whipstitched together and trimmed after the weaving is completed.

After several rows of weaving have been added, the spaces between the spokes will begin to widen and it will be necessary to add more spokes. To do that, a new length, tied on the hoop next to one of the original spokes, goes from the hoop to the last row of weaving, where it slips under a woven strip as shown in the drawing. Each time you add spokes you will need nine lengths to tie in.

The rest of the rug making alternates between weaving and adding new spokes until the ring edge is reached. Put the last stocking end to the back and untie the spokes from the metal ring to release the rug. Machine-stitch around the last row of weaving, and then trim the fringe left from the untied stockings.

9.
Stuffing and Puffs

Used nylons or pantyhose make a marvelous material for stuffing, padding, or filling. Being readily available, lightweight, and easily cut, they provide an obvious filler for such things as toys and quilts.

Nylon absorbs no water and does not get heavy, so it is unlikely to move around inside the object during the washing. You can therefore run any washable article that is stuffed with nylons through a washer-drier without fear of having the stuffing shift.

There is a grand profusion of weights, textures, and properties available among pantyhose, so you will develop preferences for certain kinds to stuff certain articles. The kind with the silky-smooth finish and shaped legs and feet retain their fullness and make a fuller, spongier stuffing, such as that required for a puff quilt. They make a loose, soft, and resilient filler, and a more even one than mesh hose or support hose. Stretch-knit hose tend to pull back into their original shapes, so they make a denser, more solid filler. Those work better when cut into smaller pieces or strips. Experience will be your guide in selecting the best kind to use for your purposes.

The stuffing may be prepared in various ways. Sometimes the hose can be used intact, either by gathering them the way you gather a stocking to slip it over your foot or by using them lengthwise and flat.

Cutting them into strips or sections gives a smoother fill to small objects. And the softer the covering material, the smaller the pieces of cut nylon must be if the surface of the article is to be smooth. Also, the more intricate the shape to be stuffed, the more important it is to cut the nylon into small pieces. Large wads can't be pushed easily into small areas.

If the covering material is felt, it is such a thick, heavy material, whole nylons can always be used for the stuffing without making a lumpy surface. Felt can also be sewn on the right side, since it isn't necessary to conceal raw edges, so felt things can be stuffed as they are sewn. That makes the projects simpler and faster to do.

If you are working with light-colored, fine fabric, you have to pay attention to the color of the stuffing. Taupe or cinnamon-colored hose tend to show through and darken white or yellow covering material. With heavier fabric, the color of the stuffing doesn't matter.

PUFFS

Nylons work beautifully when used as stuffing for puff squares, which are then readily assembled into quilts, toys, and totes.

A 6-inch square of colored fabric is a convenient and workable size to start with. This square will become the top surface of the finished piece when sewn to a 4-inch square of muslin backing. Experiment with different sizes and ratios to get the particular effect you want. The weight of the top fabric will also alter the appearance of the puff, since denim holds its shape better than, for example, a knit fabric.

Puffs are made as shown in the drawing. No basting or even pinning is required; you can sit down at the sewing machine and assemble them directly. Place a 6-inch square over a 4-inch square so that they match at one corner. Join them for a distance of about one inch, then tuck half the

Making a single puff

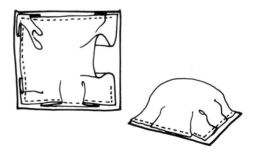

excess material of the top layer into the fold. Sew across this, making a second tuck at the other end. Turn the corner and repeat. Sew $1/4$ of an inch from the raw edge. It is not necessary that the fold or side tucks in the fabric be identical, since they puff into a kind of random pattern anyway.

When three sides of the puff have been sewn, it is time to stuff. Take one nylon stocking or cut off one leg of a pair of pantyhose and gather it as if you were going to put it on. This makes a flat, pancake shape of the nylon. Slip it into the puff, and sew the remaining side. Larger puffs may require two legs to stuff them. The weight of the material being used and the ratio of the sizes of the squares will determine the fullness. To fill with two stockings, slip one inside the other and gather them together, or stack one pancake shape on top of the other. It is not necessary to sew the two stockings together.

When a number of puffs have been made they can be joined. Place two puffs with right sides facing and stitch to join them. The line of stitching should be $3/8$ to $1/2$ of an inch from the cut raw edge. Continue adding puffs to make a row. Be sure that all seams are the

Individual square puffs are joined
into long strips for assembling into quilts or totes.

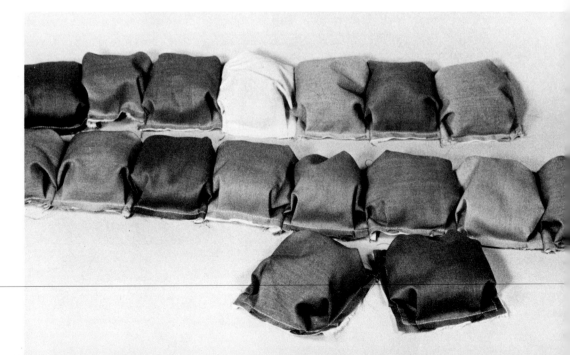

A variety of prints
in a puffed tote.
(Photo by Jean Ray Laury)

same width so that the blocks will end up being the same size. This line of stitching which joins the puffs will conceal the first line of stitching. It is always easier to assemble a number of puffs into a long strip first, and to then join the strips.

Any of a variety of materials will work well for making puffs. Denim-weight fabric looks great, especially for totes, and has been used very effectively in puff quilts. Because denim is a heavy-bodied fabric, it may require two legs for stuffing. Velveteens make a richly textured puff, though any washable printed or solid fabric can be used also. By assembling the puffs according to color, geometric patterns can be created in puff quilts.

A Trip Around the World effect can be achieved by placing a colored puff in the center and surrounding it with rows of puffs in contrasting colors.